DOGS

DOGS

COLLINS · Glasgow and London

ANIMAL
WORLD
SERIES
General Editor
David Stephen

G. P. PUTNAM'S SONS · New York

ACKNOWLEDGEMENTS

Aarons:pp.21(bottom left),62(mid right).Andia-Atlas Photo:p.65(bottom).Armez:p.64(top).Bavaria:p.75 (bottom left).Bavaria-Sorm:p.57.Bavaria-Schmidt: p.41(top right).Buzzini:pp.17,21(bottom right),22, 24,30(mid left),31(bottom),32,33(top),35(all except mid right),36(mid right),41(mid left and bottom),42 (mid right),45(bottom right),46(mid left and top right),47(mid right),48(mid right),51,52(top and bottom right),54(top),55(top right and bottom right),60,61,62(top and mid left),63(bottom right), 65(mid left),66(bottom left),67,72,73(bottom right), 75(bottom right),76(bottom),78–80,83(top and bottom right),87(top right),88(bottom).Camera Clix: pp.69(top and bottom right),87(bottom right). S.Chevallier-Atlas-Photo:p.21(top).S.Chevallier-Jacana:pp.34(bottom),42(top and bottom).La Colothèque:p.87(bottom left).C.Dautreppe-Atlas-Photo:p.88(mid left).S.Debru-Holmes-Lebel:p.20. Doumic-Atlas Photo:p.88(top).J.L.S.Dubois-Jacana:p.29(top left).E.P.S.:p.23(top),31(top). Garolla:pp.84(top),85(bottom).Holmes-Lebel:pp.15, 23(bottom),26(top left),34(top),36(bottom),37–39, 41(mid right),77.P.Jahan:36(mid left).Y.Lanceau-Jacana:pp.35(mid right),40,41(top left),42(mid left), 44(bottom).Larousse:pp.53(top right),70(bottom). Lartigue-Rapho:p.28.Lauros:pp.18–19,56(top right). Lauros-Chenil de la Maison Blanche:p.71(top left). Lebaube-Atlas Photo:p.26(top right).B.Losier:pp. 46(top left),66(bottom right),74,84(bottom),86, 87(top left).F.X.Lovat-Atlas Photo:p.16.Mac:p.9. J.Martinerie-Fotogram:p.25(bottom).Naud-Afrique-Photo:p.30(top left).Nestgen-Atlas Photo:p.27 (bottom)Okapia:p.11(top).A.Picou-Fotogram: pp.12–13.Prato:pp.36(top),43,44(top),45(top), 47(top left),53(mid left),56(top left),66(top),71(top right),81(bottom left),85(top right).Prenzel-Press: pp.29(bottom left and right),30(top right and bottom),33(bottom),45(bottom left),46(bottom), 47(top right and mid left),50(right),55(mid left), 63(top and bottom left),73(top and bottom left), 75(top),81(mid and top right).F.Prenzel:pp.48 (bottom),53(top left),68,69(bottom left),70(top),82. Rémy-Atlas Photo:p.64(bottom right).Rizzoli Archives:p.83(bottom right).Scaïoni:pp.27(top right),54(bottom),55(top left),85(top left).S.E.F.: p.65(top).Serraillier-Rapho:p.25(top).M.Silverstone-Magnum:p.81(top).J.Simon-Photo Researchers: p.10.L.Sirman:p.76(top).J.Six:p.64(bottom left). S.A.Thompson:pp.47(mid),50(left),52(bottom left). Sally Anne Thompson:Front cover.Vala-Jacana:p.49. P.Vasselet-Atlas-Photo:p.11(bottom).A.Visage-Jacana:p.56(bottom).Wells-Holmes-Lebel:p.27(left). A.Williams-Armez:pp.58–59.Ylla-Rapho:p.71 (bottom).M.Zalewski-Rapho:p.26(bottom).Zuber-Rapho:p.14.

First published in this edition 1973
Published by William Collins Sons and Company Limited, Glasgow and London, and by G. P. Putnam's Sons, New York
© 1968 Rizzoli Editore
© 1973 English language text William Collins Sons and Company Limited
Printed in Italy
ISBN 0 00 106107 0 (Collins)
SBN 399 11217 0 (G. P. Putnam's Sons)
Library of Congress Catalog Card Number: 73 79600

INTRODUCTION

How can anyone not like dogs? Of all animals, they are the most intimate companions of man, ready to serve him, and to be at his command at all times, whatever the task.

If they are the friends of man, they are even more the friends of children. They fall in willingly with all their whims and take part joyfully in their games.

Thousands of years ago, man and dog came to an understanding with each other: "If you provide me with food and shelter," the dog in effect said, I will always serve you faithfully."

Police dogs defend or guard him; sheepdogs protect his flocks; hunting dogs locate and retrieve game for him; guide dogs act as the eyes of the blind man; mountain dogs show their master the way or find him when he gets lost; sled dogs move burdens for him; coursing hounds satisfy his taste for sport. Army dogs have proved to be fine messenger dogs, stretcher bearers or parachutists.

House dogs are most agreeable companions, whose presence can become indispensable to lonely people. Always quick to respond to a call and to welcome the slightest caress, they fill an important place in the affections of man.

Pure bred dogs flatter our vanity by their beauty and pedigree, while dogs of mixed breed often make up for their lack of pedigree by their great gentleness and devotion.

For thousands of years, the dog has served man faithfully. It does not care whether its master is rich or poor; whether it lies comfortably on a cushion inside a warm room or sleeps rough outside in the cold. It relishes a good plateful of meat, but is quite satisfied with a bone to gnaw or a crust of bread —so long as the hand that feeds it is that of its master.

Surely the most extraordinary aspect of dogs is that, whatever their breed, they have retained this fundamental virtue, this loyalty to the pact that links them to man. The poodle is as faithful as the Saint Bernard, the Pekingese as faithful as the Newfoundland, the Yorkshire terrier as faithful as the Dobermann.

All these canine friends of man are to be found in this book. Each has its own personality and its characteristic form. And each has that intensely moving look that expresses so exactly all the love an animal is capable of offering.

It has often been said that the dog lives in the shadow of man. One could go even further, knowing it so well, and say that the dog *is* man's shadow.

Canidae

The family Canidae (canids), which includes our domestic dogs and related species like wolves, foxes and jackals, is one of the most characteristic in the order Carnivora. All the dogs are good, and sometimes exceptional, runners and hunters, and are well-known for their keen sense of smell. They have the typical dentition of carnivores. The enormous fangs or canines (hence the name) stand out prominently.

The canine body is slender, usually of a good size, and with a long tail. The muzzle, because of the number of teeth and the highly developed sense of smell, is more or less pointed, in contrast to the cats, which are blunt nosed, have fewer teeth and a poorer sense of smell.

Canids are subdivided (see below) into two subfamilies: *Cuoninae*, the hyaena dogs (for example *Lycaon pictus*), and the true dogs (subfamily *Caninae*). Besides the genus *Canis* (dogs and wolves), there are, in the Caninae, the genus *Vulpes* (foxes), the Arctic fox (*Alopex lagopus*), fennecs (*Fennecus* or *Megalotis zerda*), the Mexican coyote (*Thos latrans*) and African and Asian jackals (*Thos aureus* and others), as well as the South American maned wolf or *aguaré guazú* (*Chrysocyon*), the gray fox or little jackal (*Urocyon*)—both to be found on the American continent—and the raccoon dog (*Nyctereutes procyonoides*) of Siberia.

Although all canids have a·similar "doggish" look, which gives them a distinctive appearance, they are a fairly polymorphous family. Their diet is, to some extent, omnivorous but they always prefer meat, including carrion.

They are found in Eurasia and Africa as well as America.

In the Canidae, adaptation to running is prominently displayed in the bone structure of their feet. These are digitigrade, which means they walk on their toes.

1. Chrysocyon jubatus *or* Ch. brachyurus *is the aguará guazú or South American maned wolf.* 2. Canis familiaris dingo *is the Australian dingo, which is believed by some people to be a sub-species of the* common dog. 3. Canis lupus, *the wolf.* 4. Thos mesomelas *is one of the species of jackals of the Old World.* 5. Vulpes vulpes *is the common red European fox.* 6. Nyctereutes procyonoides *is the raccoon* dog *of Eastern Asia, from where it has spread to the Soviet Union and also to East Germany.* 7. Vulpes zerda *or* Megalotis (Fennecus) zerda *is the fennec.*

Their dentition is characteristic of carnivores, with a very large development of the canines and the carnassial teeth (fourth upper premolar or P4 and first lower molar or M1).

Little is known about the origins of the diverse breeds of domestic dogs (which are usually considered, zoologically, as derived from the common wolf, and are thus classified as *Canis lupus familiaris*). It is believed that the ancestral species (wild type) of the dog was a kind of wolf which, as a result of domestication and successive cross-breeding, produced hybrids. No precise details are known about the evolutionary history of the various hybrids, from which man, by a process of selection, has developed our modern breeds. These breeds can be grouped, in accordance with H. Wurmbach's system, under the following classifications:

Group I: *Canis lupus familiaris palustris* which includes the spitz (or *loulou*), pinschers, terriers and others. These are ancient breeds, originally woolly-haired.

Group II: *Canis lupus familiaris inostranzewi*, hunting dogs of the lupine type, with known subfossil remains dating back to the Bronze Age. They appear to have originated in the region of Lake Ladoga, in Western Russia about the end of the Old Stone Age.

Group III: *Canis lupus familiaris matris optimae*, a Bronze Age dog, dating back to about 3000 B.C. in Europe, from which the ancient breeds of shepherd dogs and the modern poodle probably originated.

Group IV: *Canis lupus familiaris decumanus*, sometimes huge in size, such as the great Dane (German *dogge*), the Saint Bernard and other types of guard dogs (mastiffs, etc.).

Group V: *Canis lupus familiaris intermedius*, from which many breeds of hunting dogs originated, for example pointers as well as certain types of miniature dogs (like the dachshund or "sausage dog").

Group VI: *Canis lupus familiaris leineri*, of uncertain origin, with long legs and slender shape, for example the *podenco* or Spanish hound (that is the Balearic hound), the *galgo* (Spanish greyhound), the Russian Borzoi and the Afghan hound.

As for dogs that are not domesticated, the origins of *Canis lupus dingo* are virtually unknown. It lives like a jackal in small packs of five or six animals, and is probably a *cimarrón* (a runaway dog) or a domesticated breed which reverted to the wild. Nor is much known about the pariahs—the ownerless street dogs of the Orient—semi-domesticated or completely wild, which are hybrids many times over and extremely variable. Probably cross-breeding with some species of the Asiatic jackal has contributed to their diversity.

According to a widespread and highly possible theory, domestic dogs, having originated from wolves—which hunt in packs and submit to the authority of a leader—have accepted, with domestication, the leadership of their human master. Hence the well-known "canine loyalty". The pariah dogs, on the other hand, have jackal blood in them. They are rather solitary animals, incapable of being disciplined or accepting orders, and have never been dominated by man.

CONTENTS

*Despite this picture, the Rhodesian
ridgeback is no better a climber than other
members of the Canidae family. A tree must
be very sloping before it is able to scamper
up it.*

Canidae

Canidae are medium-sized carnivores. The largest species are not as big as the big cats; nor do they possess their strength or suppleness. They have a slender body, small head and pointed muzzle; their limbs are supported on their toes; the tail is often very bushy.

The front paws have five digits, but the first toe, only partially formed, does not touch the ground or help to support the body. The hind feet have only four digits. The strong, non-retractible claws are blunt. The relatively powerful dentition consists of a maximum of 42 teeth. The carnassial teeth are well developed and the posterior molars have chewing surfaces characteristic of omnivorous animals.

In contrast to many mammals that regulate their body heat by sweating, the canids sweat very little. The evaporation of water, which is the function of sweating, takes place in the region of the lungs. This is why a dog, when it is too warm, opens its mouth and pants in order to accelerate the rythm of its breathing.

Although Canidae have very few odoriferous glands, located between the toes, they are generously provided with sebaceous glands. Those which surround the anus are particularly active and produce a fetid secretion that plays a vital role in sexual and individual recognition.

Dogs exist in every type of environment—the wildest, most desolate regions or in the proximity of towns; in the plains or in the mountains; in dense forests or in sparse scrublands, on the steppes and in the deserts. Some of them lead a nomadic existence, remaining in one place only long enough to give birth to their young and to rear them. Others dig underground shelters for themselves or take advantage of abandoned lairs.

Some species of canids are completely

10

Some Canidae lead a nomadic existence, while others dig underground hideouts or take advantage of lairs abandoned by other animals. Above: a coyote.

(Above, right)
Canidae possess neither the strength nor the suppleness of the cats, but they are all, like this wolf, superb runners and tireless walkers.

(Right)
Canidae are to be found all over the world. The lycaon is a wild African hunting dog whose general appearance is similar to the spotted hyaena.

diurnal—active only in the daytime—while some lead a semi-nocturnal life. There are others again that are totally nocturnal, spending the day in their lair or hidden in thickets, clumps of rushes or isolated ruins. They emerge when night falls, prowling around alone or in fairly large packs. In the course of their night prowling, some of them venture into villages or even towns, leaving only at the first signs of daybreak.

Some Canidae live alone or in pairs, but the majority are gregarious. Even in species where pair bonds are formed (between a male and a female) for a certain period, the couples gather together in large packs at times.

When it comes to agility, there is little to choose between the Canidae and the Felidae. Although the canids are unsuited to climbing because of their blunt claws, and although they cannot spring like the cats, they are the equals, if not the superiors, of the cats in other ways. They are all superb runners and tireless walkers. They all know how to swim, some of them with great skill. Dogs, like cats, are digitigrades, touching the ground only with their toes; but they walk in a curiously oblique manner, due to the fact that they do not place their paws one in front of each other in a straight line.

Canids have well developed senses. Their hearing can be compared to that of the cats. Their sense of smell is quite exceptional, and their sight is superior, in both the nocturnal and diurnal species.

Canids are very intelligent animals. Even the smallest species are extremely cunning. The domesticated breeds have always shown themselves to be highly intelligent. It is this intelligence that has forged a link between man and dog, and has won for the latter its privileged position among all the domesticated animals. But this intelligence is also apparent among the wild species, above all in the caution that dictates all their actions.

Canids feed mainly on flesh, and eat both freshly killed prey or animals that have been dead for some time. Indeed, they seem to show a preference for high meat. Some of them like to eat carrion, and all of them will eat mammals, birds, crustaceans, insects, honey, fruit, roots and green plants. Most of them are

Although they are omnivorous animals, Canidae eat more meat than anything else. They are not above consuming carrion and sometimes, like this jackal, fight over it with vultures.

extremely voracious and will sometimes kill more animals than they can consume.

Canids are more fertile than felids. The number of young in a litter varies, according to the species, from three to as many as twelve. The mothers care for their young with untiring tenderness.

The most powerful large Canidae, sometimes living together in very big packs, can cause considerable damage and have always, rightly or wrongly, been hunted actively by man. On the other hand, many of them, large and small, have proved to be useful in destroying rodents or in getting rid of carrion and decaying refuse.

Canidae are excellent runners and jumpers. As they are omnivorous and exist in every kind of environment, their distribution is world-wide.

The family consists of 14 genera subdivided into about 30 species. In this book, we shall look at domestic dogs.

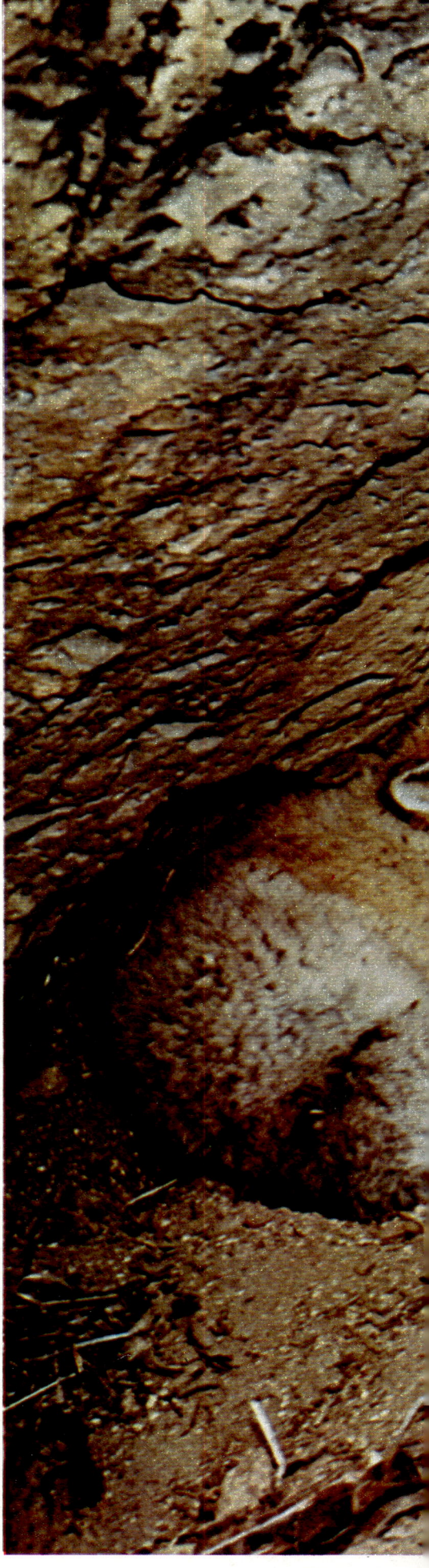

*The huge ears of the bat-eared fox (*Otocyon*) resemble those of the fennec, a much smaller African species.*

Canidae are very prolific animals. Wild species have litters of four to nine young, while domestic breeds sometimes give birth to more than twelve young. Above: young coyotes.

Domestic Dogs

The domestic Dog (*Canis familiaris*) is the most diversified of all the members of the family Canidae. One might even say that it is the most diversified of all animal species. Indeed, at first sight, it seems impossible that animals as different as a Saint Bernard, a bulldog, a Pekingese and a Chihuahua belong to the same species. Yet, even without the abundant proof of this provided by their morphology (i.e. skeletal structure, conformation of the skull, dentition, etc.), it is enough to observe their conduct to be convinced that they all belong to the same species. Dogs themselves are never deceived. To a dog, any other dog is obviously a dog, whatever its shape, size or hue. The vast number of dogs of mixed breed which populate the world provide ample evidence of this fact.

Origins

Naturalists have divided opinions as to the origins of the domestic dog and none of the theories advanced so far has been formally proved. It is agreed, however, that the dog was one of the first animals to be domesticated by man. Students of past geologic eras have, in the course of their excavations, discovered the bones of domestic dogs dating back to the Old Stone Age, and their diversity proves that there was a great variety of types even in those far-off days. Some naturalists believe that the dog first appeared in Asia, in Tibet, and emigrated from there to other continents. Others believe that several domestic breeds originated at the same time in different parts of the world.

The wolf is the most likely ancestor of the dog. It hunts in packs, like the dog, and interbreeds with it, producing fertile hybrids. The wolf has exactly the same dentition as the dog. Unlike the dog, it rarely barks.

Subsequently, crossbreeding between dogs of different origins contributed to the growth of the innumerable canine breeds, although nature, too, played a part. Adaptation to new climates and

A dog's mannerisms are nearly always conditioned by a reflex. A set-back position often indicates that the animal is on the defensive.

(Right-hand page)
In common with all gregarious species, the dog, used to living in a pack, has a strong sense of group hierarchy, which has facilitated its domestication.

(Pages 18–19)
Man has always used the dog to guard his flocks, exploiting in this way an ancestral instinct that drives the dog, as well as the wolf, to herd its prey together before choosing its victim.

living conditions has brought about a number of more or less obvious and progressive modifications, both in the appearance and in the aptitudes of the dog.

Moreover, domestication has played a vital role in encouraging the isolation of individual dogs and in controlling crossbreeding. It has partially suppressed natural selection and has enabled certain types to survive—types which, otherwise, would have been rapidly eliminated in the wild state.

Domestication

It is possible that domestication has saved the canine species from extinction. Naturalists believe that there is a correlation between the diversity of an animal species and its aptitudes for domestication. This theory seems to apply very much to the dog which has become the regular companion of primitive man—to their mutual advantage.

It was probably the remains of food that provided the first link between dog and man—dogs eating what their masters left over. The continued presence of these animals around his camp provided man with an alarm system against the more dangerous carnivores.

(Left)
Sled dogs give man precious assistance, and are still the sole method of ground transport in the frozen wilds of the Far North.

(Above and right)
Always interested in the outside world, the dog is irresistibly drawn to the limits of its territory, whether doors, windows or bars.

In the second phase, man and dog became allies in order to hunt together.

Finally, in a third phase, man used the dog to guard his flocks. This was, in fact, the exploitation of an ancestral habit. Dogs, like wolves, herd their prey before isolating the victim of their choice, usually the slowest or the weakest. Man used the dog for herding, but stopped it killing.

Finally, the dog's sexual life has played a vital role in its domestication, for if the dog's method of selecting its mate had been very complex—as is the case in many other animal species—with courtship ritual and isolation of the pair, obviously it would have had great difficulty in reproducing in captivity. Domestication is only possible so long as the animals are able to reproduce according to man's wishes.

To sum up, it would be true to say that man has domesticated a species which had the great advantage of diversity and probably lived in his proximity, sharing his food—just like the pariah dogs still to be found in the Orient.

Common Characteristics

Although their outward appearance is sometimes very different, all domestic dogs have common characteristics. Bitches come into heat twice a year, generally in spring and autumn, whereas most of the wild species come into heat only once. Mating is long and can go on for a half hour or even more. The gestation period is 63 days, with a variation of one or two days, according to breed.

Whelping sometimes lasts for several hours, the puppies appearing at intervals of from five minutes to one hour. They are born enveloped in a membrane which the bitch must tear away immediately so that the puppy can breathe. After severing the umbilical cord, the bitch eats the afterbirth, as most animals do. This placenta is rich in hormones and its ingestion helps the bitch's flow of milk.

The number of puppies in a litter varies considerably, usually from one to twelve, although the record litter is 23. In the case of large litters, the death of a certain number of the young is almost inevitable. They are born blind, under-

Puppies are born blind and under-developed. They would be incapable of surviving without the constant care of their mother.

developed and incapable of surviving without the warmth and constant attention of their mother. The latter has an extremely rich milk—as do all animals whose young are underdeveloped at birth—and she is very attentive to their needs.

During the first days after birth, the bitch hardly ever leaves her puppies, except to satisfy her needs, and then never for more than a few minutes. The first games begin towards the end of the third week. The bitch joins in the play, in which the puppies learn the strength of jaws, the pain caused by biting and the aggression of growls.

During the fourth week, the puppy begins to exhibit the submissive posture. It lies on its side, its belly sticking out, often discharging urine. After four or five weeks, the puppy is able to carry objects in its mouth and, by six weeks, it already possesses nearly all the mannerisms of its species.

(Above)
The bitch, a devoted mother for the first few weeks, becomes indifferent as soon as her puppies are old enough to look after themselves.

(Top)
In large litters, there is often a clumsy pup that is always late at feeding time, and the mother makes no effort to help it.

23

Dogs that have no contact whatsoever with human beings during these first six weeks of their life are difficult to train. Once they are fully grown, they experience difficulty in adapting themselves, make bad house companions, and always remain timid and temperamental.

The Senses

Smell is the most developed sense in dogs, although its keenness varies considerably from one breed to another. Laboratory experiments established that when puppies were deprived of their sense of smell, they were no longer capable of finding the nipples of their mother and had to be fed artificially. Later on, when they were old enough to run around, they got lost and couldn't find their way back to their bed. Once they were weaned, they relied completely upon their eyesight for feeding

purposes, and did not show any preference for meat as against bread. Finally, and this is perhaps the most curious effect, they grew up without attaching themselves to anyone.

A dog with a good sense of smell is capable of picking out one particular banknote from a pile, and of identifying its owner, provided the latter has held the note for two seconds in his hand. The most spectacular example of a dog's good nose is the way in which it can follow a scent, even when it is cut across by other scents.

Scent is the olfactory imprint left by a man or an animal on the ground he is walking over. This imprint is made up of more or less heavy, volatile molecules that can be effaced by wind, rain or heat. Smooth ground without vegetation, and easily washable, is a bad retainer of smells. For example, on a tarred road, a dog can only follow the scent successfully if the maker of the scent trail has been walking at the edge of the road. On

ploughed up, arid land, in gusty winds or when it rains, a scent trail will last only for a few minutes, whereas it can remain for 24 hours if the ground is damp, the weather calm and not too hot. In a damp meadow or wood, during calm weather, a well-trained dog can readily follow a scent trail up to 48 hours old.

Bitches usually have better noses than dogs. Their sense of smell is more subtle, although it varies with the sexual cycle. The police use male dogs for practical reasons. Whether male or female, a dog cannot follow a scent successfully unless it is accompanied by its master.

Dogs also possess a very keen sense of hearing. Whereas the human ear can hear only the lower range of frequencies up to 15,000 cycles per second, the dog's ear responds to ultrasonic frequencies up to 70,000 cycles per second.

Contrary to what one might think, dogs with raised ears do not have better hearing than other dogs. Although the hearing of dogs is superior to that of man, it appears to be inferior to that of some other animals, for example the cat.

The dog's eyesight is definitely less developed and seems to be inferior to that of the average man, but it can see better than man in the dark. It can distinguish hues but its perception of shapes is rather rudimentary.

Food

Since the Canidae are carnivores, meat is naturally the first choice of all domestic dogs. But they will eat carrion and meat that is high.

A carnivore in the wild state, when it kills a herbivore, often begins by eating the intestines which contain partially digested plants. These supply the carnivore with vital vitamins which would otherwise be lacking in a diet consisting solely of flesh. Similarly, the food of the domestic dog should include a certain proportion (about a third) of products of vegetable origin—so that it is, in fact, an omnivorous animal.

Contrary to what was once believed, fats and offal are not at all harmful to the dog so long as they are taken in small quantities. Milk, although the composition of cow's milk is rather different from

The dog serves man in innumerable ways but at the same time is totally dependent upon him. In contrast to the cat, the dog is usually incapable of finding its own food.

that of a bitch, may also be included in a dog's diet in reasonable amounts. Fish is good too—provided the bones have been removed beforehand.

As for food of vegetable origin, this comes mainly in the form of cereals, but bread, pastry, biscuits, porridge, rice, oats and barley can only be assimilated properly in small quantities. Green vegetables, preferably raw, can contribute valuable vitamins to a dog's diet.

Sugar, an energy-giving food of vegetable origin, should be given only to dogs making great muscular efforts. If given to less energetic dogs, it might have harmful effects on their health.

Communication

It is in their mannerisms that all domestic dogs most closely resemble each other. Whatever their apparent differences, they all communicate with each other and transmit information which is of interest to them personally. Vocal signals are the most obvious ones.

The posture of dogs is a more discreet method of communication but just as expressive. Dogs can show their sympathy or their antipathy by the position of their tail, which can be raised, waved to and fro, or placed between the legs. The head and ears can also be moved expressively.

Finally, dogs communicate by spurts of urine which they distribute generously in their tracks. These indicate the age of the animal, its sex, its social status, etc. When given complete freedom, dogs will lead a structured social life based on a strong hierarchical system. Each dog will follow, at least once a day, the scent of the urine trail marked by its fellow dogs. It may cover several miles on its tour and take several hours. Sometimes two animals will make part of the journey together.

The male dog usually marks its passage by urinating on the trail already in existence. The anal glands, too, are a very rich source of information. They identify the individual. This explains the habit dogs have of sniffing each other under the tail.

The domestic dog, being incapable of providing for its needs by itself, has been dominated since the earliest days

of its relations with man by its need to have a master who will assure it security, shelter and food, and to whom it can attach itself. Attachment and fidelity are the basic charactcristics of the domestic dog. It is from these characteristics that the desire arises to retain the secure place it enjoys next to its master, a desire that reveals itself in two other ways: the display of aggression and courage. These bear no relation whatsoever to the size or strength of the dog.

Morphology

The variations in structure and shape of the different breeds of domestic dog are so extensive that they have had an effect on certain factors such as the keenness of the senses and the duration of life. Small dogs often live longer than large ones. Weight can vary from two to four pounds (Chihuahua) up to 290 pounds (Saint Bernard), and the height can vary

(Top)
In spite of their diverse appearance, all domestic dogs belong to the same species, and the innumerable breeds are merely variations within that species.

(Right)
Hostility between cats and dogs is often maintained by man. In reality, these supposedly natural enemies often get on very well together.

from six to thirty-five inches.

The relative size of head, body and limbs has given rise to the classification of dogs into two main categories: dolichomorphic (elongated dogs like the greyhound) and brachymorphic (stocky dogs like the bulldog). Harmoniously-developed dogs like the French pointer constitute a third category: mesomorphic dogs. Finally, a fourth category should be added: anacholimorphic dogs, or bassets, whose body is normal in size, but whose legs are reduced to half the normal length.

It is, above all, the shape of the head that enables one to distinguish a particular breed. Dogs can be dolichocephalic (narrow, elongated head) or brachycephalic (short, wide head).

The profile, the length of muzzle, the shape and position of the ears, the fronto-nasal depression or stop, the shape and pigmentation of the eyes and nose are described in detail in the portrait-sketches of each breed or standard. The ratio between the length of muzzle (from the tip of the nose to the stop) and that of the skull (from the stop to the occipital apophysis) varies from 1/1 (setters and pointers), 1/2 (boxers), to 3/4 (cocker spaniels). In some breeds of terriers, the ratio is superior to the unit, the length of muzzle exceeding that of the skull.

According to the way they are set, the ears of a dog can be erect, semi-erect or pendant. The tail is equally important. In certain breeds it is docked, while in others it should be long. Finally, the hair

can be long, medium length, short, silky, soft, woolly, rough, smooth, wavy or curly.

The Many Uses of the Domestic Dog

In addition to the traditional uses the dog has been put to, which we shall be discussing when we come to the different breeds (hunting dogs, guard dogs, sheepdogs, and house companions), man has found innumerable ways of making use of the dog, many of which have now fallen into disuse.

Today one never sees dogs turning a spit or drawing water, and the majority of the spectacles in which they took part

in former days, such as fights against bears or bulls and rat-catching competitions, are now forbidden for humanitarian reasons. But greyhound racing continues to draw huge crowds of spectators in many European countries.

Greyhound Racing

These races fall into two categories. Racing dogs against live hares, called coursing, takes place either in the open air (open coursing) or inside (park coursing). This coursing, run in heats, is very popular in England and Spain. Greyhound racing with a mechanical hare takes place on an oval-shaped track so that a large audience can follow the

(Top, left)
Since ancient times, man, for financial gain, has taught the dog to perform balancing and other tricks.

(Top, middle)
Coursing hounds specially trained for racing, usually greyhounds, can go faster than a galloping horse over a short distance.

(Above)
The dog can be highly trained for military purposes and still has a part to play in modern armies, in spite of improved, highly technical equipment.

action. Greyhound racing has become highly popular over the last 50 years or so. In England there are more than 150 licensed greyhound stadiums. In France, the only stadium in existence (since 1935) was closed in 1951, after the authorities, at the instigation of the horse-racing associations, had withdrawn its betting licence, without which it could not survive.

Coursing hounds are usually greyhounds, whose speed can exceed 40 miles per hour, from a standing start—which is faster than the speed of a racehorse over the same distance. In Algeria, the dogs used in organized racing are sloughis, which are not so fast but have greater endurance over longer distances. In English-speaking countries, there is

quite a lot of interest in whippet racing, and large crowds can be drawn.

Sled Dogs

Dogs are also used to transport goods. This use, which was, at one time, quite widespread, has virtually died out, except in the polar regions where no other means of transport has yet replaced them. The sled dogs of the Far North belong, by and large, to two types: the eskimo dog, found in Greenland and Canada, and the Samoyed, originating in Siberia. The sleds are very low and light. The dogs are attached by leather harnesses of varying shapes and styles.

(Above)
A team of sled dogs becomes virtually inseparable with a strong sense of group hierarchy, the leading dog being undisputed leader.

(Top, right)
Dogs specially trained to act as guide dogs for the blind wear a special type of harness.

(Above)
In the old days, dogs were often harnessed to carriages, but this practice, due to abuses arising out of it, is now illegal in most parts of the world.

27

In a team of dogs, one animal is the undisputed leader. These groups form virtually indissoluble units, even during the summer when, in the absence of snow, the dogs may be allowed to run free to find their own food for themselves.

A team of eight to ten dogs, moving at a brisk pace, can cover a distance of 40 miles a day drawing a load of 650 pounds, and a team of 12 to 15 dogs, at a walking pace, can pull a sled loaded with as much as one ton in weight for 15 hours a day.

Army and Police Dogs

The dog has been employed from

earliest times for military purposes and today it is still used in a number of ways in modern armies. It can carry munitions and materials from one place to another. Messenger dogs serve as a means of liaison when other methods are not available. Ambulance dogs search for the wounded. During World War II, the belligerents trained dogs, carrying an electromagnetic mine, to throw themselves under enemy armed cars and cause them to explode. The escort dog follows its master on his rounds; the scout dog reconnoitres an area, attacking anyone it meets; the watchdog warns of approaching danger by its posture, without barking. Dogs have also been used for tracking and detecting mines.

In police forces, dogs are specially trained for defensive purposes and for searching for missing persons. They are never assigned to the maintenance of order; nor are they used for purposes of attack.

Guide Dogs for the Blind

In 1915, the first headquarters for the systematic training of guide dogs for the blind was established in Germany. Subsequently, similar places were set up in Switzerland, the United States, Italy, England and Belgium. The dogs used for this purpose are usually German shepherd dogs. Boxers are also used.

Although dogs have been domesticated since time immemorial, they still retain the instincts of their ancestors, and love to gallop through the countryside.

Hunting Dogs

In the days when man's only weapons were clubs and flint axes, and when hunting was almost the only source of food, the dog became an important ally. To the hunting team of man and dog, the dog contributed its sense of smell, its speed and its powerful teeth. In those far off days, the dogs killed what they hunted and man benefited. Since the invention of firearms, however, dogs no longer kill their prey, except in sports like fox hunting and otter hunting. But, as every shooting man knows, there is still no substitute for the nose of a good hunting dog.

Greyhounds (or Coursing Hounds)

The greyhound is one of the most ancient breeds whose origin goes far back into recorded history. The perfect greyhound type is portrayed on ancient Egyptian monuments dating back more than two thousand years before the Christian era. The ancient Greeks and Romans, and the kings and nobility of the Middle Ages, used these hounds. The great speed of the greyhound is still used today in hare coursing and track racing. In France, coursing with greyhounds has been illegal since 1844, and the only racing stadium was closed in

1951. So the breed has been relegated to the status of a household pet. In many other countries, however, including Britain, coursing is legal, and many greyhounds are specially trained to hunt the hare. Track racing is a growing sport in the United States.

All greyhounds are large, slender hounds with long legs and muzzles, narrow, deep chests, hollow bellies and powerful muscles. Most of them have little or no sense of smell and hunt mainly by sight, abandoning pursuit of the quarry as soon as it disappears.

The greyhound. This is the best known, the most widely distributed and very probably the fastest of all the

1. Since the age of the cave man, the dog has always hunted with man.
2. Whippet.
3. Greyhounds.

coursing hounds. Its hind limbs are longer than its fore limbs. It has long, powerful jaws. A greyhound running at top speed can reach down and break the backbone of a hare with a single bite. It is the ideal racing dog. The hair of the greyhound is fine and dense, and the coat can be of any hue. The height of an adult dog is about two feet, and weight is 65 to 70 pounds for the dog and 60 to 65 pounds for the bitch.

The whippet is a miniature greyhound, standing up to 22 inches tall to the withers and weighing about 22 pounds. The breed was probably derived from a cross between the greyhound and fox terrier.

The deerhound is a very ancient Scottish breed, once used for hunting deer. It has medium-long, coarse hair. The most popular shade is bluish-gray, but any shade is permissible. Deerhounds measure up to two and a half feet at the withers and weigh up to 100 pounds.

The Irish wolfhound is believed, by some authorities, to be the ancestor of the deerhound. Now very rare, it is a very big breed, measuring at least 32 inches in height and weighing 120 pounds.

The borzoi, or Russian greyhound was used by the Russian nobility in Czarist days for hunting the wolf. The Revolution led to the dispersal of the great aristocratic kennels, but many people in England began to breed borzoi

about that time. The borzoi is at least 28 inches tall and weighs 75 to 105 pounds.

The saluki or Persian greyhound weighs about 45 pounds. The hair is short on the body, but long on the thighs and tail. The dog is from 23 to 28 inches.

The Afghan hound is the most ancient breed known. It can be traced back to 3000 B.C. in Egypt. According to legend, the dogs taken aboard the Ark by Noah were Afghan hounds. How the breed was introduced to Afghanistan, nobody knows, but it was brought from there to England by British Army Officers. The Afghan has long, profuse, curly hair.

The sloughi was introduced to North Africa from Arabia by the Muslim invaders. The Arabs consider it the only noble dog, all other breeds being impure.

The galgo is a Spanish greyhound that closely resembles a sloughi and is probably descended from dogs taken to Spain by the Arab invaders. The coat is usually fawn or brindled.

The Balearic hound originated in Ibiza. Unlike other greyhounds, it has erect ears and a well-developed sense of smell. The coat can be smooth, rough or long. The Spaniards use it as a gun dog, allowing it to course hares that have been missed or have risen out of gunshot.

30

1. *Sloughi.*
2. *Saluki.*
3. *Wolfhound.*
4. *Borzois.*

5. *Afghan Hound.*
6. *Deerhound.*
7. *Balearic Hound.*
8. *Galgo.*

5

6

7

8

1

2

3

4

5

6

7

8

32

Scenting Hounds

Unlike greyhounds, which hunt by sight, the hounds of this group rely entirely on their noses. They bark loudly when they scent their quarry and follow its scent trail at high speed.

The Saint-Hubert hound originated in the Ardennes. It has an extremely acute sense of smell. The breed is extinct in France, but can still be found in England under the name of bloodhound. This is a large dog with a sad expression, measuring 26 inches tall and weighing 88 pounds. Because of its acute sense of smell, the bloodhound has been much used in crosses to produce new breeds or to improve breeds already in existence.

The blue basset of Gascogny is a Saint-Hubert hound adapted to the hot sun of Southern France. It is blue-coated instead of black.

The petit bleu is a miniature variety, measuring less than 23 inches tall.

The Poitevin is a dog with attractive markings in three shades which can be considered the typical modern French hunting hound.

The Griffon Nivernais is a shaggy breed with a sad expression, mainly used for hunting the wild boar.

The Griffon Vendéen is one of the most intelligent of hound breeds, still much used for the hunting of boars and hares in the Vendée district of France. It is a bold and persistent hunter.

The English foxhound is the typical English pack-hound. It had been bred to a high pitch of excellence for hunting foxes. The coat is usually either white, black and tan or lemon and white. The standard foxhound measures up to 23 inches at the withers and weighs about 65 pounds. Because of its strength, speed, powers of endurance and keen sense of smell, the Englsh foxhound can safely be described as the finest example of successful dog breeding.

The harrier is used in England for hunting hares. It is smaller and slower, but more finely drawn than the fox-

hound. Harriers are very popular in America where they are used for tracking in thick cover. The most popular size is 19 to 21 inches.

The beagle is an ancient English breed. It is a hare hunter, small in size and slow enough to be followed on foot. Because of the modern fashion for long-distance hunting on horseback, the beagle is losing some of its popularity as a pack-hound. On the other hand, it is becoming extremely popular as a household dog. It is an elegant, jaunty little dog with three hues in its coat. It measures up to 14 inches tall at the withers.

The basset is a hound whose height has been reduced by selective breeding. As the basset's legs are short, it can hunt through and under low cover in pursuit of its quarry. The *basset Vendéen* is used for hare hunting in a region where thick hedges make it impracticable to use horses and where the *griffon Vendéen* is too fast to be followed on foot. The *basset fauve de Bretagne* is very active for its small size. The *basset Artésian-Normand* hunts on its own instead of in a pack.

1. *Griffon nivernais.*
2. *Briquet or Griffon Vendéen.*
3. *Basset Artésian-Normand.*
4. *Poitevin.*
5. *Beagles.*

6. *Griffon Pointer.*
7. *Blue basset of Gascogny.*
8. *Basset Griffon Vendéen.*
9. *Saint-Hubert.*
10. *Foxhounds.*

Gun Dogs

The pointer is a gun dog trained to quarter ground in search of game and to stop and point with its nose when it finds it. When ranging over a small area, it trots; when casting over a wide area, it gallops. When a pointer stops, it stands perfectly still, with its legs immobile and its nose pointing in the direction of the scent. All its muscles are tense and the tail is held straight in line with the body, while the dog waits for its master to shoot the game.

French Gun Dogs

The Braques are short-haired dogs with white coats, heavily freckled or patched. Their name is derived from the German *brachacker*, meaning hilly or uncultivated land, the kind of terrain in which these dogs are highly skilled in hunting. All Braques are sturdy dogs with long, drooping ears. They have a large head, a flat skull and a wide,

square muzzle. The upper lip overlaps the lower jaw. The long tail is sometimes docked. Height varies from 20 to 25 inches.

The French pointer is a strongly built dog with coarse, thick hair, and is the breed found south of the Garonne. The *Bourbonnais pointer*, which has been improved by crossing with foreign breeds, is more elegant in appearance. Its tail is docked to a stump, and its white coat is speckled with dark purple. Its height does not exceed 23 inches. The *Dupuy pointer*, derived from a cross between the greyhound and the French pointer, can reach a height of 27 inches. The *Saint Germain pointer* is a cross between the English pointer and a Braque. It has a dull white coat with patches of orange. The coat of the *Auvergne pointer* has bluish-black patches and flecks which give it its more popular French name of *Bleu d'Auvergne*

Spaniels are gun dogs with longish, silky hair which can be smooth or wavy. Spaniels have a long head, with a well-defined stop, a straight muzzle and

feathered hanging ears. Very often, the tail and legs are also feathered. Height ranges, according to breed, from 15 to 25 inches.

The French spaniel which had almost died out by the end of the 19th century, has today regained its popularity. It has a white coat, marked with brown, and is notable for its even temper and keen sense of smell. The *Picardy spaniel* is a variety of French spaniel, specially adapted for hunting on marshland. The *Pont Audemer spaniel* is derived from a cross

34

1. *French Pointers.*
2. *Saint Germain Pointer.*
3. *Auvergne Pointer.*
4. *French Spaniel.*

3

4

5

6

7

between the Picardy spaniel and an English or Irish water spaniel. It is an intelligent, energetic breed, and hunts equally well in deep water or marshland. The *Brittany spaniel* is 17½ to 20½ inches tall. It has a short tail, and its white coat is marked with red or chestnut patches.

Griffons are gun dogs that resemble pointers in size and bone structure, but they have wiry coats.

The barbet is a very ancient breed, considered by some authorities to be the ancestor of all dogs with long, woolly hair, for example, the poodle and the *Briard (Brie shepherd dog)*. It is a very courageous dog, superb in the water, used exclusively for duck shooting.

5. *Griffon fauve de Bretagne.*
6. *Griffon Pointer.*
7. *Brittany Spaniel.*
8. *Picardy Spaniel.*

8

British Gun Dogs (pointers, setters, spaniels, retrievers)

The pointer was taken to Britain from Spain by the British army at the beginning of the 18th century. Rigorous selective breeding over the years has produced a type widely considered to be the greatest of all gun dogs. The pointer's well-defined stop gives it a distinctive profile. The pointer stands 28 inches tall at the withers.

English spaniels can be divided into two types—land spaniels for hunting on dry land, and water spaniels used on marshland. Spaniels are extremely active dogs, but they are not as effective at pointing as the true pointers. They are used mainly for flushing game or driving rabbits out of cover.

The cocker spaniel is the best known of all the land spaniels. It was originally used for flushing woodcock, but is now very little used as a worker. Its intelligence, good nature and small size have made it very popular as a house dog.

The field spaniel is usually black, with a flat, silky, glossy coat, which falls in silky fringes on the legs and ears.

The springer spaniel is the largest breed. The *clumber spaniel* is the heaviest and stockiest in build, and can weigh as much as 65 pounds. In spite of its great size, it is a calm, docile dog, with a very good nose and great powers of endurance. The coat is white, with lemon markings. *The Sussex spaniel* is distinguished by its beautiful mahogany-red sheened coat. It may be the most ancient spaniel breed.

There are two varieties of water spaniel. The English water spaniel, after a period of eclipse lasting several centuries, was revived in the 19th century, probably as a result of crossing the French *barbet* with the English springer. It is a strong, rather heavy dog, well suited to working in deep water. The *Irish water spaniel* has a very distinctive appearance, and may well be the product of a cross between the poodle and the Irish setter.

1. Cocker Spaniels.
2. English Pointer.
3. Irish Water Spaniel.
4. Springer Spaniel.
5. Spaniels in action.

(Right-hand page)
Laverack setter and Irish setter.

(Pages 38–39)
Pack hounds rely on their good noses to track down the game that they hunt.

Setters are large spaniels whose name is derived from the verb 'to set', meaning to lie down. Many setters have retained this habit of remaining immobile, in a reclining position, as their ancestors used to do.

The Laverack setter (the English setter) is named after the famous 19th century breeder, Edward Laverack, and a dog was considered to be of the best if it was the Laverack strain. The Laverack is a very loyal, affectionate dog, and hunts well over all types of ground. The silky coat is marked and flecked in varying degree. Plain coats are not popular.

The Irish setter is the most ancient British gun dog. It has a more slender body than the Laverack, and the richness of its red coat gives it such an elegant appearance that it has now become more of a household dog than a hunting dog.

The Gordon setter is black and tan. It is a bigger dog than the Irish setter, without being too heavily built, and is an excellent gun dog.

Retrievers have a special function. While most gun dogs are hunters that will carry game to their masters, the retrievers find and carry, but do not hunt. The well-trained retriever sits quietly until game is killed and it is ordered out to carry it back. Finding wounded game is part of its work. The modern system of driving game from cover means that pointers and setters are no longer needed in the field. So first-class retrievers are becoming more and more popular.

The golden retriever is one of the most handsome types. Its golden-brown coat is waterproof, a great advantage to a dog that works much in water. This breed stands 23 to 24 inches tall. It was produced by crossing a caucasian shepherd dog, bought by Lord Tweedmouth at a circus, with a bloodhound.

The Labrador is the most popular of all retrievers. It came originally from Newfoundland where the sailors used it to retrieve fish that had escaped from their fishing hooks. It is a large, powerfully built dog, standing up to 24½ inches tall and weighing 60 to 75 pounds. Its short, dense, flat coat resembles that of the otter. The coat is usually jet black,

(Left)
The job of a pointer, like this German short-haired pointer, is to flush out the game; but it also retrieves it once it has been killed.

1. Golden Retriever.
2. Labrador.
3. Gordon Setter.
4. Irish Setter.
5. Laverack Setters.

although yellow and tan varieties of this breed are becoming popular.

The flat-coated retriever is a black or mahogany dog, produced by crossing the Newfoundland with the Irish setter, while the *curly-coated retriever*, also black or dark red, has an astrakhan-like coat of crisp curls, and was produced by crossing the English water spaniel with the poodle and the Newfoundland.

Finally, there is the *Chesapeake Bay retriever* which is the largest of the breeds, weighing 65 to 75 pounds. This specifically American breed is unequalled for duck shooting. It is a cross between the Newfoundland and the otter hounds, and has a waterproof coat and webbed feet. It is said to be capable of retrieving up to 200 ducks in one day from the freezing waters of Chesapeake Bay in the Northern United States.

German Gun Dogs

The German short-haired pointer or *kurzhaar* is a very ancient breed, probably of Spanish origin, which has been successfully crossed with an English pointer to give it a more elegant appearance. Dogs of this breed measure up to 23–25 inches long at the withers. The coat, usually brown or black pied, is inherited from the English pointer. *The Weimar pointer* is as big as the German short-haired, but lighter in build. It is the only gun dog with a silvery-gray coat.

The Korthals is a pointing griffon, bred in 1870 by a Dutch hunter called Eduard Korthals. It has a very wiry gray-blue coat with large patches.

The Munsterlander (Munsterland spaniel) is very like the Brittany spaniel, except for its more elongated head. It is a reliable gun dog that retrieves well and which can be used with a pack of hounds. It stands about 20 inches tall at the withers, but there is a giant variety, measuring up to 25 inches. The larger variety is black and white.

Italian Gun Dogs

The spinone is a griffon that can be

42

1. *German Short-haired Pointer or Kurzhaar.*
2. *Munsterland Spaniel.*
3. *Elkhound.*
4. *Korthals.*
5. *Wire-haired Fox Terrier.*

used for all types of hunting. The feet are finely webbed. Height varies from 25 to 27 inches. The most popular coat is brown, but white is also acceptable.

The bracco or Italian pointer may well be the ancestor of most European pointers. This is a large breed, standing up to 27 inches tall and weighing 90 pounds. There is a smaller variety, up to 24 inches and 60 pounds. Braccos have a white coat with orange patches.

Nordic Gun Dogs

The Norwegian elkhound is a large spitz of Scandinavian origin. It is one of the most ancient breeds. Fossilised skeletons of the elkhound have been found,

dating back to the Stone Age, which are identical with the structure of the present-day breeds. The elkhound has a keen sense of smell and is able to wind elk from a great distance. Elk hunting is severely restricted nowadays, but the elkhound is still very popular as a companion dog.

The Finnish spitz is tawny and resembles a fox. It has a pointed muzzle, mobile ears and lively movements. It prefers to hunt feathered game, especially grouse and blackcock, in the Finnish forests. The Lapps think very highly of it, but it is not a prolific breeder and is rather rare even in its own country. English and American breeders are becoming very interested in it.

Terriers

Terriers were bred to go to ground, into burrow or earth or set, to bolt or kill the occupants. More often than not, dogs went down to bolt fox or badger, both powerful and courageous animals, so the terrier is primarily a fighting dog. All terriers have to be small enough to enter such dens and, at the same time, big enough and strong enough to defend themselves in the underground tunnels. They have powerful muscles and strong jaws and short or docked tails. The coat may be smooth or wiry. These little dogs, if not kept under control, can be rowdy.

cropped, which gave it a slender, delicate profile. Ear cropping is now illegal in Britain. In the United States, standard ears may be cropped, but not toy ears. Height is 16 inches and weight about 15 pounds.

The toy terrier is a toy variety of the Manchester. Although it measures no more than ten inches at the withers, this is a true terrier, full of courage, and it does not hesitate to attack rats as big as itself.

The black-and-tan terrier is a strongly muscled dog with pointed muzzle and protruding eyes. It has slender legs, large chest and a hollow belly. The ears are either erect or partly drooping. The name black-and-tan terrier is no longer used. The breed is now usually referred to as the Manchester terrier (see above).

The West Highland white terrier is a small white Scottish breed, full of vitality and courage. It has erect ears, a vertical tail and alert eyes. Originally, the West Highland was a white cairn terrier, the whites turning up in litters with puppies of other hues. By careful selection, the present well-defined breed was established.

The Skye terrier is named after the Hebridean island where it originated. Probably the best known of all terriers between the 16th century and the end of the 19th century, it has become less popular because its long coat needs much care and attention. The Skye is as short-legged as the basset-hound, and is solidly built. It weighs 20 pounds and stands up to ten inches tall at the shoulder.

The Dandie Dinmont terrier derives its name from a character in Sir Walter Scott's novel, *Guy Mannering*. The character in the novel owned a pack of these dogs. The breed was first produced by a Scottish farmer, and is a good hunter and first-rate ratter. Its arched skull has a topknot of silky, soft, creamy-white hair. The rest of its coat is rougher and darker. The height is 8 to 11 inches.

The Scottish terrier. Although there

British Terriers

The fox terrier is still used in England for fox-hunting. It has to be small enough to go to ground and big enough to be able to follow hounds on foot. Smooth-haired or wire-haired, the fox terrier is white, with black or tan patches. It is full of vitality. Maximum weight is 20 pounds; maximum height 15½ inches.

The Manchester terrier is probably derived from a cross between a black-and-tan ratter and a whippet. At one time the breed always had its ears

1. Smooth-haired Fox Terrier.
2. Fox Terriers in action.

2

is a fawn version of this terrier, the black is the best-known and most popular. The Scottish terrier works on the surface of the ground, and was not used for going to earth after foxes. Its head is long in relation to its stocky body, and its muzzle is profusely covered with hair. The tail, which is naturally short, is carried upright. The breed has been almost ruined by fashion, and bitches now have difficulty in giving birth to their pups.

The Boston terrier, of American origin, is primarily a house dog rather than a hunting dog, and we shall be discussing it later on.

The cairn terrier, by contrast, and despite its small size, is a true hunting terrier. Even when kept as a household pet, it cannot resist being a hunter. The cairn originated in the Hebrides and was bred to hunt foxes, marten and wildcat. It has a face like a fox. The cairn's coat is usually tawny, although it can be almost black. Weight is about 14 pounds.

The Yorkshire terrier is one of the smallest, and is classified as a house companion or toy dog.

The Airedale terrier originated in the

3. Dandie Dinmont.
4. Skye Terrier.
5. Scottish Terrier.

45

Aire Valley in Yorkshire. In contrast to the Yorkshire terrier, it is the largest of the terriers, and is often referred to as the "king of the terriers". It measures 18 to 19 inches at the shoulders, and weighs about 50 pounds.

The Lakeland terrier formerly hunted with foxhound packs in the North of England. After World War I, breeders became less concerned with its working abilities and concentrated on producing a show type of agreeable appearance and alert expression.

The Welsh terrier is of medium size—between that of an Airedale and the Lakeland terrier which it closely resembles. Like the Airedale and the Lakeland, the Welsh is derived from the English black-and-tan terriers which became extinct at the turn of the present century. The Welsh has a long, powerful head, flat skull and strong jaws. It has practically no stop. In common with all terriers, it is lively, with great powers of endurance, and has a powerful scissor bite. Its hair is hard and wiry, the coat black and tan or gray and tan. It measures up to 15 inches tall and weighs between 18 and 20 pounds.

The Sealyham terrier was bred in Sealyham, a rural district of Pembrokeshire, by Captain John Edwards, about 1850. His aim was to produce a terrier courageous enough to confront any wild animal. For this purpose, he selected certain terriers and matched them against polecats, rejecting all those animals that showed reluctance to fight. The Sealyham has been accepted as a separate breed since 1910, but the modern breed has much shorter legs than the original. The rough, white coat should be marked only on the head. The breed is very popular in the United States.

The Bedlington terrier is one of the oldest breeds of officially accepted terriers. This dog hails from Northumberland and has a white, silky topknot derived from a Dandie Dinmont ancestor. It has no stop. Its legs are long and slender, its coat is woolly. It measures up to 16½ inches and weighs between 17 and 23 pounds.

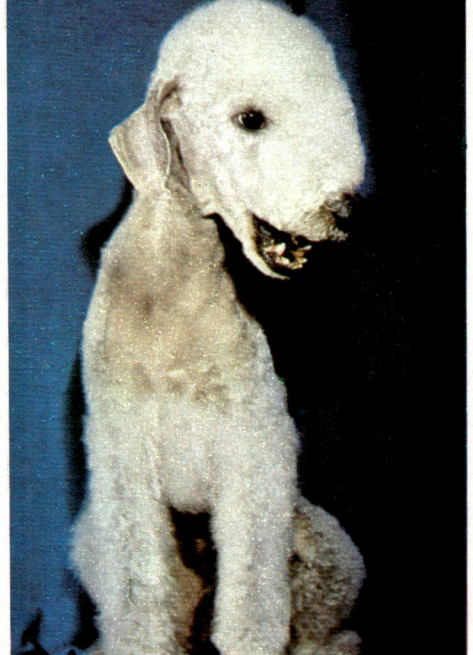

The bull terrier in its modern form dates back to the middle of the 19th century. Its exact origin is uncertain, but the white dog was produced by crossing with terriers of mixed breed which, at tht time, were used for bull-baiting. The bull terrier is an intelligent, tough and extremely courageous animal. It has an egg-shaped head with no stop, small black eyes, small ears, a muscular body and a thick neck. Its long, tapering tail is carried horizontally. The coat, mainly white, is smooth and lustrous, but there are some animals marked with black. The standard height is up to 24 inches, but there is a miniature variety, weighing less than 22 pounds, whose height does not exceed 14 inches.

The border terrier has been known as a type since the 17th century, but was not officially accepted as a breed until 1920. It was bred in the border area of England and Scotland. The coat can be reddish-brown, tawny, gray and tan or blue and tan. Height is up to 12 inches and weight up to 15 pounds.

The Norwich and the Norfolk terriers. Norwich is the County Town of Norfolk, and the town and county breeds are identical, except in one point. The Norfolk has hanging ears; the Norwich has erect ears. In fact, in the United States the Norfolk is called a Norwich terrier with drop ears. Both are small, stocky, short-legged dogs, derived from the Irish terriers that were used for hunting badgers in Norfolk.

The soft-coated wheaten terrier is probably the oldest of the Irish terriers, although it was not officially accepted as

46

1. Toy Terrier.
2. Sealyham Terrier.
3. Bedlington Terrier.
4. Cairn Terrier.

5

7 8

9

a breed until 1943. It measures up to 20 inches in height, and maximum weight is 44 pounds.

The Irish red terrier looks like an over-sized wire-haired fox terrier, with a reddish coat. It is good-natured with human beings, but quarrelsome with other dogs—a fault shared by many other terriers. Because of its quarrelsome nature, it was frequently involved in dog fights; hence its nickname of "red devil". It measures up to 18 inches tall and weighs between 24 and 26 pounds.

The Kerry blue terrier is a large Irish breed, probably derived from a cross between the Irish red and the soft-coated wheaten terrier, with a dash of gadhar—an ancient breed of sheepdog that is now extinct. Although the Kerry blue has been in existence in Kerry since the 19th century, it was not officially accepted until 1920. It is a multi-purpose

dog and, like the Irish red, it has a reputation as a fighter. The coat is either silvery-gray or steel blue, with abundant long, silky and rather curly hair. Weight ranges up to 37 pounds, and height to 18 inches.

The Australian terrier, which is very popular in Australia, closely resembles the cairn terrier of Scotland from which it is descended by cross-breeding with Norwich and Yorkshire terriers. It is one of the smallest hunting terriers, weighing only 11 pounds, and standing ten inches tall, but it is bursting with vitality and high spirits. The tail is docked, the ears erect or folded. The coat is blue and tan or reddish-brown.

German Terriers

The German hunt terrier (jagdter-rier) resembles the Welsh terrier in general appearance. It is a strong dog,

with a long, narrow head, arched skull, and only slight stop. Its ears are "V" shaped and folded, so that the tips fall forward like those of the fox terrier.

The dachsbracke resembles the dach-shund, but is a much larger breed, standing up to 16 inches tall at the withers. It is built to hunt over all kinds of ground. The domed skull has a clearly marked deep furrow down the middle.

The dachshund or teckel is not a small dog, but a basset with a normal-sized body. Only its legs are shorter. The short legs, originally the result of a mutation, have been assiduously main-tained by selective breeding. The dach-shund is a brave and tenacious dog, and is classified as a terrier because it hunts fox and badger underground. It also hunts above ground and with a pack. There are six varieties.

5. Kerry Blue Terrier.
6. Airedale.
7. Yorkshire Terrier.
8. Bull Terrier.
9. Welsh Terrier.

47

The smooth-haired dachshund has always been the most popular type. Its coat is dense, short, glossy and flat. All, hues, except white, are permissible. The most popular colours are tawny or black and tan. The body should be as long and low as possible, the limbs thick and the head slender. Weight is from 15 pounds but should never exceed 24 pounds.

The long-haired dachshund is considered, in Germany, to be the most ancient variety. Its soft, shiny, wavy coat resembles that of the Irish setter, and forms a thick fringe on the tail.

The wire-haired dachshund has never been as popular as the other two.

The three miniature varieties of dachshund have the same coats as the standards, and they are extremely popular nowadays as house dogs. Any miniature dachshund should weigh less than 11 pounds.

1. Short-haired and long-haired Dachshunds.
2. Long-haired Dachshund.
3. Wire-haired Dachshund.
4. German Hunt Terrier.

Watchdogs

The classification of watchdogs is inevitably a rather arbitrary one, since most dogs have a natural tendency to defend the person, home and possessions of their master. Many sheepdogs and house companions make excellent watchdogs; but certain breeds are more predisposed than others to this kind of work because of their vigilance, their bravery and their strength.

There are two distinct categories: mountain dogs and large mastiff-type dogs.

Mountain Dogs

Mountains dogs are all fairly closely related to one another. Some breeds have avoided extinction only by being crossed with other breeds with similar characteristics.

The Tibetan mastiff is possibly the progenitor of all mountains dogs. Aristotle described it, and Marco Polo spoke about it after returning from his visit to the Grand Moghul. It was, it seems, an enormous animal—sometimes as large as a small donkey—and of remarkable strength and ferocity. Its modern descendants are not so large, but they can still measure up to 33 inches tall and weigh more than 165 pounds. They have a big, wide head, a square-shaped muzzle and small drooping ears. The long, rough hair is black, sometimes marked with tan-coloured patches.

The Pyrenean mountain dog should not be confused with the Pyrenean sheepdog—often called the Pyrenean dog—which is much smaller. The Pyrenean mountain dog is a very large animal. It is often mistaken for a Saint

Mountain dogs all bear a close resemblance to each other. They are large dogs with thick hair and pendant ears, whose ancestor was probably the Tibetan mastiff. This is a Pyrenean mountain dog.

49

Bernard, because of their similar size. It probably originated in the region of Ariège where, for centuries, it protected the herds against wolves and bears. Its hind feet have double dew claws (rudimentary inner toes). Its height varies from 28 to 32 inches but the weight never exceeds 132 pounds.

The Leonberger is a German dog which bears the name of its town of origin in Wurtemberg. It is the product of a cross between the Saint Bernard and the Newfoundland. It is as big, if not bigger, than the Saint Bernard. Golden to reddish, it usually has a black mask.

The Saint Bernard, although not very common, is world famous. Everyone has heard of the dogs reared by the monks of the hospice of the Great Saint Bernard in the Swiss Alps, which was founded in the 10th century by Saint Bernard of Menthon. Thanks to their keen scent and sense of direction, they have saved hundreds of people lost in the snow. One famous dog, named Barry—which is now on exhibition (stuffed) in a Berne museum—saved the lives of forty people before being killed by the forty-first who mistook it for a wolf. The Saint Bernard measures a minimum of $27\frac{1}{2}$ inches and certain males weigh up to 220 pounds. There is a long-haired and a short-haired variety. The coat is white and rusty-red.

The Bernese mountain dog measures from 23 to $27\frac{1}{2}$ inches in height. Its long hair is black and tan with white on the chest. The paws, forehead and the end of the tail are often white.

The Newfoundland is probably rel-

1. *Saint Bernard.*
2. *Bernese Mountain Dog.*
3. *Newfoundland.*
4. *Leonberger.*

ated to the Saint Bernard, but it has not yet been established how it reached Newfoundland, where it must have been crossed with the Labrador. From its general appearance, its size and its thick coat, it is clearly a Molossian dog. While the Saint Bernard is the traditional mountain rescue dog, the Newfoundland is the sea rescue dog. In its native country, people exploit its enormous strength by making it pull carts and haul in the fishing nets. Its coat is black, lustreless and waterproof. The Newfoundland measures 28 inches tall and weighs up to 150 pounds.

The Portuguese mountain dog looks like the Pyrenean mountain dog. It is the national watchdog of Portugal. It is a massive-looking animal, wolf-gray of coat with a pale coffee belly.

3

4

1

2

3

52

Mastiff-type Dogs

There is a large number of dogs in this group, more widely differentiated than those in the mountain dog group. The mastiffs include large dogs with rather long muzzles as well as large dogs with crooked feet and flattened muzzles. The two types are certainly descended from different ancestors.

The great Dane or German mastiff is a dog that was once used for boar-hunting. It is a massive animal with a very noble bearing. It measures at least 30 inches and weighs 120 pounds. It is affectionate with its masters, very gentle with children, but suspicious of strangers. Because of its poor sense of smell, it has acquired the rather exaggerated reputation of not being able to recognize its master at night. Its smooth and glossy coat can be a plain tawny, black or blue, striped or harlequin (black patches on a white background).

The mastiff is the most ancient of the European *doggen*. Its enormous size very

nearly led to its extinction and, at the end of World War II, only a few rare specimens of this dog were to be found in England. Thanks to the determined efforts of dedicated breeders, the breed now seems to be safe from extinction. The mastiff should measure at least 30 inches tall and weigh 165 to 175 pounds.

The bull mastiff is probably the finest of all watchdogs. From its dual ancestry it has inherited the vitality of the bulldog and the strength of the mastiff. Although not so massive as the latter (it measures 25 to 27 inches tall and weighs about 110 to 130 pounds), it is faster-moving and just as vigilant. It has a wide head with prominent jaws, a muscular body and smooth coat. Because of its keen sense of smell, the bull mastiff was very highly thought of by gamekeepers who used it for catching poachers.

The dogue de Bordeaux has a broad, wrinkled head and its truncated muzzle gives it a fearful appearance. It has a thick, muscular neck, deep chest and broad back. The coat is usually tawny with red or black mask. Its height

ranges from 24 to 30 inches, and its weight can be as much as 110 pounds.

The Italian mastiff measures 24 inches in height. It has a massive head with a short, very broad muzzle. Its body is long with sturdy legs and short, dense hair. It has a gray coat with black ears and muzzle or, alternatively, its coat can be plain brown.

The boxer is a German dog, first bred in 1895, which is descended from a drover dog called *bullenheisser*, meaning

1. Dogue de Bordeaux.
2. Harlequin Great Dane.
3. Bull Mastiff.

4. Great Dane or German Mastiff.
5. English Mastiff.
6. Italian Mastiff.

53

"bull-biter". Selective breeding has refined and softened its character. It is slimmer than other mastiff-type dogs, but has the size, temperament and speed of a police dog. In fact, it is used primarily for this purpose in Germany. Its height should range from 22½ to 25 inches and it weighs 65 pounds. The coat is tawny or brindled.

The bulldog hides a tender and affectionate nature behind its rather unprepossessing appearance. It is descended by selection from the mastiff. In the 17th century it was a most formidable-looking dog, used in bull-baiting. The prominence of its jaws gave it a very powerful grip. Today it has almost lost its pugnacity. Its nose has become so short that it can scarcely breathe; its jaws have lost much of their prominence, and thus their gripping strength; and it is too heavy to be active. It has a short body, thick neck and prominent chest. The loins are higher than the withers, the forelimbs stronger than the hindlimbs. Its height ranges from 12 to 16 inches, and its weight is about 50 pounds. Intelligent, docile and peaceful, the bulldog is a calm animal which often refuses to fight with other dogs. When it does, however, it is a formidable adversary.

Pinschers

Pinschers are dogs of German origin which have certain characteristics in common with terriers. Their name, in German, means "pincher". They can be either smooth-haired or rough-haired. The former are the true Pinschers, while the latter (which used to be called *griffons d'écurie*—stable griffons—in France) are schnauzers.

The Dobermann is the best-known of the pinschers. It was first bred in 1860 by Jules Dobermann, but its ancestry is not known. It is an extremely fine and elegant dog. It has a long head, muscular body and hollow belly. Its coat is short and smooth, black and tan, or brown and tan. It has a docked tail. Ear cropping is illegal in Britain, but in the United States ears are commonly cropped. Used in many countries as an army or police dog, the Dobermann measures

1. Boxer.
2. Schnauzer.

26 to 28 inches and weighs 77 pounds.

The schnauzer is an ancient German breed. It is a sturdy, active and energetic dog, rather like a terrier in appearance, but not so aggressive. Like the terrier, it is an excellent ratter. There are three varieties, classified according to size. The standard schnauzer measures less than 20 inches. It is a stocky animal with a docked tail and cropped ears (illegal in Britain). In the United States both cropped and natural ears are permitted for show dogs. It has dense, rough hair which is pepper-and-salt or black and forms bushy eyebrows, a moustache and beard. The giant schnauzer or *kiesenschnauzer* can measure up to 27½ inches. In Germany it is often used as a police dog, but outside its native country it is virtually unknown. There is also a miniature schnauzer or *zwergschnauzer*, a dwarf version of the standard, which does not exceed 12 to 14 inches in height.

Spitz

The spitz have a broad skull, pointed muzzle, a rather pronounced stop, erect, triangular ears, a bushy tail curled over the back, abundant hair on a woolly undercoat, a solid bone structure and a stocky body. Some breeds are used as sheepdogs, some as hunting dogs. For the present, we shall be dealing with those spitz that have the special qualities required to make a good watchdog. It should not be forgotten that good watchdogs are to be found in every breed.

The grand loulou originated on the Baltic coast. The Germans call it spitz and the Russians *Laika*, meaning "barker". It is, in fact, a very alert, watchful dog which barks frequently. The French name loulou comes from the word *loup*, meaning wolf, although there is no

3. Bulldog.
4. Miniature Schnauzer.
5. Dobermann.
6. Spitz.

proof that wolves ever interbred with these dogs. The grand loulou measures from 18 to 20 inches tall. Its hair is rough and abundant, with a thick, woolly undercoat. Its almond-shaped eyes are very deepset, and the nose and nasal mucous membranes are black. The coat can range from white to black, but it should always be whole.

The Keeshond is the Dutch version of the spitz, named after a popular reformer, William Kees who, in the 17th century, made the spitz the symbol of his movement. In the old days, these dogs were used mainly as watchdogs on board the barges which sail up and down the Dutch canals. The triangular head is surrounded by a thick, bushy ruff and the eyes are encircled with light hair which looks like spectacles. The coat is fairly dark gray and height ranges from 18 to 20 inches. The Keeshond, which becomes very attached to its master but is distant with strangers, is a superb watchdog, for it warns of the approach of intruders without attacking them.

The chow chow is a Chinese spitz with certain distinctive characteristics. It is the only spitz to have a bluish-black tongue, wide muzzle, small, short ears and a straight hock. Its thick hair forms an opulent-looking ruff. It is either red or black, while a cross between these sometimes produces a very pretty blue shade. Its height should be about 20 inches, and the body very well-built and thickset.

1. Keeshond (Dutch Spitz).
2.–3. Chow Chow.

(Pages 58–59)
These three collie bitches are daughter, mother and grandmother.

The Saint Bernard is the largest domestic dog. It is a descendant of the great Molossian dogs brought back from India by Alexander the Great and discovered in Macedonia by the Romans. These fierce dogs were used by the Romans when crossing the Alps through the Great Saint Bernard Pass.

Sheepdogs

To be able to do its job properly, the sheepdog should be of medium build, smaller than the sheep it is guarding. Many sheepdogs belong to the group of "wolf dogs", so called because they have erect ears, elongated muzzles and thick hair. Today, when wolves and bears have virtually disappeared, the task of the sheepdog consists mainly of leading the animals to their pastures and of preventing them from straying. The largest species, formerly used to protect the flocks against attackers, are often nowadays used as guard or police dogs.

French Sheepdogs

The Beauceron is a large, short-haired dog that can measure up to 27 inches tall. Its coat may be plain or marked, but it is usually black and tan, in which case the dog is known as *bas-rouge* (red-stocking). Its head is elongated and its ears are usually cropped.

The Briard is a breed that goes back to the 12th century. Its long, rough and shaggy hair is similar to that of a goat. The ears are cropped. All plain hues are permissible, except white. Its height is from 27 inches.

The Picardy sheepdog is a medium-sized dog, whose general appearance

1.–2. Briard or Brie Sheepdog.
3. Beauceron or "Bas-Rouge" (red stocking).
(Left)
The intelligence and vigilance of the Alsatian, or German Shepherd, makes it a superb watchdog.

61

ruff. The curling tail resembles that of the loulou.

resembles that of a griffon. It has a strong muzzle with beard and moustache, powerful jaws, and erect ears. Its legs are long and muscular, its hair dense, medium-length and rough to the touch. Its coat is gray or tawny, marked with white on the chest and feet.

The Pyrenean sheepdog should not be confused with the large Pyrenean mountain dog. It is a small, active and sturdy dog which does not measure more than 20 inches in height. Its head, with wedge-shaped muzzle, resembles that of a bear. The ears are cropped. The tail is sometimes naturally short but more usually docked. The hair is abundant, especially on the hind-quarters, and is sometimes slightly wavy. Its coat is tawny, gray or harlequin. Because of difficulties of communication between the different valleys of the Pyrenees, there are small local variations in the breed which, slight though they may be, are enough for them to be given

individual names such as the *berger de Labeda*, the *berger de Bagnères*, the *chien d'Arbazie*, the *berger de Saint Béat*, the *berger d'Azun* and so on. A smooth-faced variety also exists, whose muzzle is more pointed and which is slightly larger than the standard size.

The Languedoc sheepdog looks like a smaller version of the Beauceron. There are a number of varieties called *berger de Camargue, berger de la Crau, berger des Garrigues* or *berger de Larzac*. Their coat is often black and tan, and occasionally harlequin. They hardly ever measure more than 20 inches up to the withers.

The Savoy sheepdog, although not a recognized breed, is a more standardized type than the Languedoc sheepdog. It is a medium-sized dog (18 to 22 inches) and its weight does not exceed 55 pounds. It has a strong muzzle, pendant ears, and medium-length hair forming a

Sheepdogs of Other Countries

The Algerian sheepdog is often called the Kabyle dog or douar dog. A douar is an Arab encampment. Its extraordinarily keen sense of smell enables it to pick out the sheep in a flock belonging to a different douar from its own. It is a rather large dog with medium-length hair, usually white, although it is occasionally marked with fawn patches. It has erect ears, a bushy tail and a long muzzle. Because of its uncertain temper, it is not a very popular dog.

The Alsatian or German shepherd dog is also known as the wolf hound. Because of its intelligence, constant alertness and docility, the Alsatian has been used as a police dog all over the world. It is also the dog most commonly used as a guide dog for the blind. In the Alps, where it guides the rescue teams towards mountaineers trapped by an avalanche, the traditional keen sense of smell of the sheepdog is exploited—the sense that enables it to indicate to its master the location of a sheep buried under the snow. There are three varieties, classified according to length of hair, but easily the most popular is the short-haired variety. All coat colours are permissible, although white dogs are less in demand. The Alsatian can measure up to 26 inches.

1. *Picardy Sheepdogs.*
2. *Malinois.*
3. *Pyrenean Sheepdog.*
4. *Alsatians.*

Belgian Breeds

The groenendael is a Belgian sheepdog with long, wiry black hair. Its shape is rather similar to that of the Alsatian, but it is smaller in size, rarely measuring 24 inches tall and weighing less than 55 pounds.

The tervueren is identical to the groenendael apart from its hue which is a tawny-reddish-charcoal. Interbreeding occurs so frequently between tervuerens and groenendaels that their genetics have become somewhat mixed, so that two black groenendaels could produce tawny-red tervueren puppies and vice versa. It has also been known for groenendael and tervuren puppies to be found in the same litter.

The malinois is a short-haired Belgian sheepdog. It is tawny with a black mask.

5. *Alsatian.*
6. *Tervueren.*
7. *Groenendael.*

63

1

3

British Breeds

The old English sheepdog bears such a close resemblance to the French Briard that it is very possible that they shared a common ancestor in the far distant past. Its placid-looking appearance is deceptive because it is a very active animal which makes a fine watchdog as well as a fine sheepdog. It has a short tail, often none at all. All shades of gray are permissible. Most of these dogs stand taller than 22 inches at the withers.

1. Old English Sheepdog.
2.–3. Collies.

2

5

The corgi is a small Welsh dog, two varieties of which are now accepted: the *Pembroke* and the *Cardigan*. The former is noted in Britain as a personal choice of Queen Elizabeth II. It has a short tail, either natural or docked, whereas the Cardigan, rather larger in size, has a long fox-like tail. Their height is about 12 inches and their weight no more than 30 pounds.

The border collie should not be confused with the border terrier, although they both originated in the border counties lying between Scotland and England. It is a very special and valuable breed, and without a doubt the most widely used of British sheepdogs in all areas of the world where flocks of sheep need looking after. It measures about 20 inches, weighs 53 to 55 pounds, and is usually black and white, or black, tan and white. It has acquired such a high reputation for its intelligence and its extraordinary powers of resistance, that it is exported to all countries where livestock are reared, often accompanied by a recording of the orders it is accustomed to obeying.

The collie is the best-known of the British sheepdogs. Selective breeding has refined its shape, and its appearance has gained while its natural talents have been lost in the process. Nowadays, it is mainly used as a house dog. Its very elongated head with almost non-existent stop resembles that of the greyhound. A short-haired variety exists, but the long-haired collie is by far the more common. The hair is dense and rough with a close-growing and soft undercoat. It forms a profuse mane around the neck, and the legs and tail are fringed. The head is close-cropped. All coat hues are permissible but strongly contrasting markings are preferred. Its weight can be as much as 75 pounds and height up to 26 inches.

The Shetland sheepdog is a "collie in miniature" which measures 13 to 16 inches at shoulder. Because of its size, it is popular as a house companion.

Other Breeds

The Maremmano is very common in central Italy. It is a large, white dog similar to the French Pyrenean sheepdog, although smaller in size.

4. Maremmano.
5. Shetland Sheepdog.
6. Pembroke Corgi.

6

The Bergamaschi herder is an Italian sheepdog. It is a large, shaggy-haired dog which bears some resemblance to the French Briard. Bushy hair falls over its eyes and forms a beard and moustache. It has a large head with a well-defined stop and small ears covered by long fringes. The most common coats are gray and tawny yellow. The Bergamaschi herder measures up to 25 inches.

The Abruzzi sheepdog, often confused with the Maremmano, is closer to the wolf dog type of sheepdog. Its thick coat is usually white, but occasionally biscuit.

1. Bergamaschi Herder.
2.–3. Puli (Hungarian Sheepdog).

The **Appenzell sheepdog** is a Swiss dog used mainly as a guard dog. It is about 22 inches in height, strong without being massive. It has short black hair marked with white or tan. Its small ears are pendant, while its tail, covered with thicker hair than the rest of the body, is carred curled over the back.

The **Dutch shepherd dog** belongs to the wolf dog type. Its height does not exceed 23 inches. Its ears are erect and pointed, its tail is carried low, and its narrow head has only a slight stop. Its coat, often brindled, can be long or short.

The **puli** is a Hungarian sheepdog of medium size that is a fast-moving persistent worker. It has pendant ears, and thick, rather long hair, especially on the muzzle and tail. All hues are permissible and its average height is about 17 inches.

The **komondor** is the largest and possibly the oldest of the Hungarian sheepdogs. On the vast plains of Hungary, its thick, white, fleece hair gets tangled and matted, which protects it against cold and, formerly, against wolf bites. Its height exceeds 25½ inches.

The **Gos d'Atura or Catalan sheepdog (herder)** possesses a magnificent long, silky coat, slightly wavy; its silvery shade is due to a mixture of black, white and tawny hair. The ears are usually cropped and the tail docked.

The **kelpie** is an Australian sheepdog probably descended from the collie and the dingo. Its height is about 24 inches. It has the erect ears, intelligent expression and pointed muzzle of the spitz. Its thick black hair is of medium length.

The **Owtscharki or Russian sheepdog** is one of the largest of the sheepdogs. Its height is over 32 inches. Its thick, abundant and woolly hair is inclined to matt and falls over its large, intelligent eyes. The ears are normally cropped and the tail docked. The most common hues are gray, tawny and grayish-white.

The **Lapland sheepdog** watches over

the herds of half-wild reindeer belonging to the nomadic tribes which travel the desolate empty spaces stretching across the north of Finland, Sweden and Norway. It is a typical spitz measuring 16 to 20 inches in height, with a stocky body, a triangular-shaped head and its tail carried in a curl over its back. Its thick coat can be all shades of gray, but it is never white.

The **Phuquoc dog** lives on the island of the same name in the Gulf of Siam. It probably bears a closer resemblance to the wolf than any other type of sheepdog. Its height is about 24 inches and it has a fawn coat, darker on the nose

4. Flanders drover dog.
5. The Great Swiss drover dog.

67

and back. Its hair is very short with a ridge of erect hairs along the spine.

Drover Dogs

The function of drover dogs, in theory, is to drive cattle from one place to another, but, in fact, most of them are efficient at guarding flocks of sheep.

The Flanders drover dog originated in the south of Belgium and in northern France. It has a rough, tousled coat, a hairy muzzle and measures from $23\frac{1}{2}$ to $27\frac{1}{2}$ inches. Its imposing appearance, combined with its courage and strength, makes it an excellent guard dog. It has erect ears, its tail is reduced to a

stump and its neck is thick. The most common hues are fawn and gray. It can weigh as much as 80 pounds.

The Roulers drover dog is a close relative of the preceding dog, but is larger in size. Its coat is black, sometimes with gray paws.

The Ardennes drover dog looks like the Pyrenean sheepdog. It should not exceed 24 inches. Its hair forms a beard and moustache on the muzzle. All coat hues are permissible.

The Rottweiler is a German drover dog descended from the dogs used by the ancient Romans to drive the herds destined to feed their legionaries. Today

it is used as an army or police dog. Its coat is usually black with yellow markings or yellow with black markings.

The great Swiss drover dog measures at least 26 inches tall. Because of its strength, it has been used for transport. It has rather short, wiry hair, pendant ears and a well-built body.

The kuvasz is a Hungarian drover dog. About 26 inches tall, it has a fairly long muzzle, a slight stop, slightly pendulous lips and small, pendant ears. Its hair is rough, abundant and rather long. While it is never curly, it may be slightly wavy. Intelligent, loyal and affectionate, the kuvasz is fairly popular in the United States.

(Above)
Drover dogs, which provide valuable assistance to the cattle herders, are large, powerful dogs, rougher and not as slim as sheepdogs. This is a Rottweiler.

House Companions

In this group are included all those dogs that no longer perform any kind of work or service either because they are too small to be able to do anything or because they are no longer needed for the work for which they were originally bred. The poodle is a good example. It was bred as a hunting dog, and may well stage a come-back in this capacity some time in the future if a sufficient number of them can prove their abilities. Other breeds have been diverted by fashion from their original work and turned into pets. Among these are cocker spaniels, Alsatians, many terriers and hounds. But this is a classification that must be subject to frequent revision. For example, some dogs that used to be classified as pleasure dogs, or simply as pets, have become reclassified as workers. This is certainly true of the Keeshond and the grand loulou, both of which are now officially accepted as watchdogs. But many pets are also guard dogs in the sense that they guard their master's possessions by instinct.

Although they are not, strictly speaking, house companions, there are many hunting dogs, watchdogs and sheepdogs that make delightful companions. 1. Wire-haired Fox Terriers. 2. Dachshund. 3. Schnauzers.

The poodle originated in Central Europe and is descended from the French barbet. It was formerly used as a gun dog, especially for hunting water fowl in the marshes. Its main duty was to swim through the water in search of the game which had been shot down. This was why hunters used to clip the hair on its hindquarters. When it got sodden with water, the thick, woolly fleece impeded the dog's movements when swimming. Today this habit of clipping them is still retained.

The coat of the poodle should be a plain black, brown or white, or a mixture of these. In English-speaking countries, some intermediary shades are permissible, known as blue, gray, champagne and apricot. The poodle has a long head with slight stop. Its nose is well-developed with wide nostrils and its eyes are very deep-set and slightly almond-shaped. The rather long ears hang very flat and are covered with long, wavy hair. The body is well proportioned with a straight back and rounded croup. The tail is docked to a third of its length. The forelimbs should be perfectly straight.

There are three varieties of poodles, classified according to size. In Great Britain, the large poodle measures more than 18 inches in height, the standard between 14 and 18 inches, and the miniature poodle measures less than 14 inches. The large poodle is often mistakenly called the royal poodle, but this name applies only to the corded poodle.

In the United States the classifications are standard poodle (over 15 inches at the highest point of the shoulders), miniature (in excess of 10 inches up to 15), and toy (10 inches and under).

1.–3. Poodles.

The French bulldog comes from very lowly origins. It was first bred near the end of the 19th century by the butchers of the slaughter-houses at la Villette quarter of Paris, who had a passion for dog-fighting. When first introduced into England in 1894, it unleashed a passionate controversy. It was criticized for its large, erect ears and its domed forehead, so different from the traditional English bulldog. Since the English breeders, however, had not managed to produce a good miniature bulldog, the French breed was finally accepted.

This docile dog has a squarish head, well-defined stop, and a short, wrinkled nose. The teeth and tongue should not be visible and the eyes should not protrude. The large, wide-apart ears, broad at the base, rounded at the tips, are carried erect. The legs are straight, the tail usually short, twisted and carried close to the hindquarters. A medium-size, tapering tail is also permissible and should not be docked. Its coat may be brindled, fawn, white or brindled and white with black round the eyes. Its weight should not exceed 30 pounds.

The Boston terrier is an American dog which, despite its name, bears a much closer resemblance to the bulldog than to a terrier. It has a round head with a short muzzle, but without the wrinkles of the French bulldog, and it is slimmer in build. The small ears are cropped to a point, and the tail is straight and tapering. Its coat is brindled, marked with big white patches on the head, the chest and hindquarters. Boston terriers are classified into three varieties, according to weight: lightweight—under 15 pounds; middleweight—15 to under 20 pounds;

4.–5. French bulldogs.
6. Boston Terriers.

heavyweight—20 to 25 pounds, the last being the maximum official weight. This dog was enormously popular in the United States during the first quarter of this century.

The dalmatian, despite its name, is unlikely to have originated in Dalmatia on the west coast of Yugoslavia. Although it is sometimes called the "little Dane" because of its coat which resembles the harlequin coat of the great Dane, it is not a mastiff-type dog at all, but related to the pointers. It is intelligent and easy to train, and the Americans use it as a police dog.

The dalmatian is a medium-sized dog that measures 19 to 23 inches in height and weighs 55 pounds. It has a flat, rather wide skull, a long muzzle, and pendant ears. The tapering tail is of medium length, and the legs are straight and sturdy. It has short, dense and glossy hair. The basic coat is pure white, marked with black or dark brown spots. The spots should be evenly distributed, widely spaced and clearly defined. These spots do not appear until two or three months after birth.

The Italian greyhound or levrette probably comes from the Middle East, but its origins lie far back in history. The patricians of Ancient Rome admired its delicate shape and grace, and it was popular at all the European courts, where it posed with its noble masters for the most famous painters. Its height should ideally be about 13 to 15 inches. Its maximum weight is seven pounds. Its body is an exact replica in miniature of the large greyhound, with its arched chest, well-tucked up belly and long, slim legs with bulging muscles. It has a long head with a slight stop. The very thin, tapering tail is carried low. The pendant ears are small and set rather high. The coat is as soft as satin and the Italian greyhound is one of the few dogs that need to be protected against cold in winter. Its coat is usually plain black, tawny or gray, sometimes marked with white on the chest and feet.

The pug (carlin) probably originated in China, whence Dutch navigators brought it to Europe in the 17th century. The pug or carlin is a small dog (12 inches), solidly built with a large head, short muzzle and very heavy wrinkles. It has prominent eyes, small ears and a thick neck. The tail should be curled as tightly as possible and carried over the

back. Its short, glossy hair has no scent,
—an advantage in a house companion.

Hairless dogs are totally, or almost
totally, devoid of hair. They are to be
found in various parts of the world,
mainly in hot, damp climates where
they can live without experiencing too
many difficulties of adaptation. All
breeds are rather rare and bear a certain
resemblance to small terriers. Some
varieties have a tuft of hair growing on
the top of the head, and occasionally
at the end of the tail. This seems to be
due to mutations caused by selection.

Hairless dogs are usually small in size.
The largest of the Mexican *Xolos* does
not exceed 35 pounds in weight. The
smallest, the Chinese hairless dog, has a
globular-shaped head and measures
barely ten inches. The Antilles hairless
dog has a cinder-gray skin with black
legs and muzzle. Others, like the African
sand dog, are marked with black patches.
It appears that pigmentation varies according to the season and the degree of
sunshine. All these dogs are considered
to be alert and affectionate. They are
very sensitive to cold.

2

3

4

1. *Dalmatian.*
2. *Levrettes or Italian Greyhounds.*
3. *Carlin or Pug.*
4. *Mexican Xolos.*

Miniature (Toy) Spaniels

Most of the miniature spaniels are very ancient breeds. Little is known of their origins but probably they are descended from standard spaniels and were reduced in size by selective breeding. They can be classified into three groups: the continental, the English and the oriental.

Continental miniature spaniels probably originated in Flanders. There are two varieties: One with drop ears, and the other, the papillon, with erect ears. Since all spaniels have drop ears, there can be no doubt that the first variety is the oldest, while the papillon was the product of a later cross with a loulou. Both these varieties are small dogs, with a height of less than 11 inches and weight not exceeding seven pounds. They are very lively, playful and good-natured. The head is small with profusely fringed ears and strong teeth. The fringed tail is medium-length and carried gaily. The hair is thick and silky, sometimes slightly wavy but never curly. It is short and smooth on the face, but forms a rich-looking ruff. All hues are permissible, but the face of the papillon should have a long, white blaze shaped like a butterfly, the ears representing the wings.

British miniature spaniels are called toy spaniels. They were produced, in the second half of the 17th century, by crossing continental miniature spaniels,

probably coming from Spain, with oriental dogs given to Catherine of Braganza, the wife of Charles II, by missionaries. There are five varieties of the descendants of these toy spaniels, all very closely related to one another. *The King Charles spaniel* is black and tan. It measures from 10 to 13 inches in height and weighs from 7 to 13 pounds. It has a very short, turned-up nose, and domed skull. The tongue should not be visible. Its pendant ears are profusely fringed, as are its legs and tail. The tail is carried straight in line with the back. Its hair is silky but never curly. *The Prince Charles spaniel* has black and tan markings on a white ground. *The Blenheim* also has a white coat, but with chestnut markings, while *ruby* has a plain, mahogany coat. *The cavalier King Charles spaniel*, although a close relative of the preceding British toy spaniels, is slightly different. In 1926, an American offered a prize to the English breeder most successful in breeding a dog bearing the closest resemblance to the ancient toy spaniel, as represented in the paintings of Sir

1. and 4. Papillon dogs.
2. Cavalier King Charles Spaniel.
3. King Charles Spaniel.

Edwin Henry Landseer (1802–1873). As a result of this competition, a much larger spaniel than the King Charles was produced. Its face is not so flat and its shape is more slender. It can weigh up to 18 pounds and it has the same coat as the King Charles: black and tan, tricolour, white and chestnut, or mahogany.

Oriental miniature spaniels belong to extremely ancient and probably related breeds, but little is known about their origins.

The Pekingese (Pekinese). Thanks to its well-built body and powerful muscles, the Pekingese is a very hardy dog, and this has probably contributed much to its popularity. It was in 1860 that British soldiers first brought back Pekingese to Europe, after sacking the Summer Palace in Peking during the Boxer Rising.

The Pekingese is very short-legged and its height rarely exceeds ten inches, but it can weigh up to 18 pounds. It has a short muzzle, protruding eyes, fringed,

1.–2. Pekingese.

(Right)
Toy Poodle.

Page 78: Tenerife dog.
Page 79: Toy Spitz.

The Tibetan toy spaniels are difficult to differentiate from one another. Some of them are called "chrysanthemums" because of their thick, abundant hair, while others bear a closer resemblance to griffons. Most of them have drop ears and all of them have long hair, curly or flat.

The Shitzu or Shih-Tzu measures about 8 to 11 inches. It is lively, frisky and very courageous. It has the short muzzle of the Pekingese, but its very long and profuse hair is straighter and falls over its eyes. The tail is carried curled over the back. All hues are permissible, but white foreheads and tail tips are especially popular.

The Lhasa or Tibetan Apso bears a close resemblance to the Shitzu, but it is a little smaller. Its big head has a characteristic beard. Its intelligence and audacity make it a good watchdog in spite of its small size.

The Tibetan spaniel was probably the product of a cross between a Pekingese and a Tibetan terrier. Its head is longer than that of the Apso and less hairy. Its legs are slightly crooked. The flat hair

pendant ears and a long body, the fore-limbs being heavy and twisted. Its hair is long and flat, forming a profuse mane on the neck and shoulders. The tail is carried in a loose curl. The Pekingese has a gay, affectionate nature.

The Japanese toy spaniel or Chin-Chin first appeared in Europe at the end of the 19th century. It resembles the Pekingese, to which it is undoubtedly related, but it is more slender. It has straight legs and delicate bone structure. Its silky, abundant hair is usually black and white, but it can also be white and rust-red. Its muzzle is always white. It measures up to 11 inches, and weighs five pounds.

(Left)
Pug dogs.

1. *Lhasa or Tibetan Apso.*
2. *Japanese Toy Spaniel.*
3. *Shitzu.*
4. *Tibetan Terrier.*

forms a mane and the tail is carried gaily. All hues are permissible.

The Tibetan terrier bears a closer resemblance to a spaniel that to a terrier. It is very much taller than the other Tibetan breeds and ranges from 14 to 16 inches. It weighs 30 pounds, twice as much as the other varieties. According to the standard, it should look rather like a very small version of the old English sheepdog.

Toy Flemish dogs are called "Ladies' dogs" in their native country.

The Brussels toy griffon, first appeared in Belgium a little over a hundred years ago. Descended from a wire-haired ratter, it is a small, sturdy dog. Its large, round head, its bulging forehead, its very short nose, its dishevelled hair and its little beard give it a rather ape-like appearance. The erect ears are docked to a point. The legs are straight, perpendicular and of medium length. The coat can be black, russet-red or black and tan. Its height varies from 10 to 11 inches and it weighs nine pounds.

The Brabançon is a short-haired Brussels toy griffon.

The schipperke is classified by some writers as a watchdog, although its height does not exceed 14 inches and its weight is up to 18 pounds. Its name in Flemish means "little captain" and, ever since the Middle Ages, it has performed the same function in Belgium as that of the keeshond in Holland: it guards the barges. The fashion for docking the whole tail is said to date back to the 15th century, and this, combined with its fox-like head, gives the schipperke its characteristic appearance. It has a wide forehead, a pointed muzzle, and only a slight stop. The small, triangular-shaped ears are set on high and carried erect. It has straight legs, muscular loins and low hocks. Its rough, thick, black hair forms a profuse mane. The largest of these dogs can measure up to 14 inches at the withers and weigh 20 pounds; the smallest weigh only seven pounds.

The Affenpinscher is a small German griffon which could be the ancestor of

1

1. Brabançon Toy Griffon.
2. Schipperke.
3. Affenpinscher.
4. Miniature Pinscher.

the Brussels toy griffon, to which it bears a close resemblance. Due to its hairy appearance, its alert expression and its amusing postures, it is known as the monkey griffon, the monkey terrier or the little devil. It is not as stocky as the Brussels toy griffon and has longer legs and a larger head. It has a well-defined stop, bristling moustache and bushy eyebrows. Its muzzle is short and its tail docked. Its body is covered with medium-length, rough, dull hair, which is either gray or reddish-brown. Animals with pale coats often have a black mask. Height should not exceed $10\frac{1}{4}$ inches and its weight nine pounds.

The Pinscher in a miniature Dobermann, although they are probably not descended from the same ancestry. It is an elegant and thoroughbred dog with a wiry, highly-strung body, cropped ears and perfectly straight legs. Its height ranges from 17 to 19 inches. It has short, dense hair and its coat is black and

more common. It has a long head, flat skull and only a slight stop. The ears are cropped to a point and the tail is usually docked. The back is straight, the belly hollow, the forelimbs straight. Its coat is black and tan, brown and tan or plain mahogany.

Spitz

Spitz have a triangular-shaped head, erect and pointed ears, thick hair and a curled tail. We have already discussed the Finnish spitz, a hunting dog, as well as the keeshond and the chow chow, both of which are classified as watchdogs.

The Pomeranian spitz is a German dog which is descended from the great white Pomeranian spitz and can weigh up to 13 pounds. It has a domed skull, a well-defined stop and short ears which are always carried erect. As with all spitz, its eyes are slightly almond-shaped. The tail is bushy and the hair abundant, forming a mane on the neck and fringes on the legs. All plain hues are permissible, but the most popular are pure white, cream, gray and black. Markings are acceptable on this spitz provided that they are evenly distributed.

The miniature spitz serves as an excellent example of what breeders are capable of achieving by selective breeding in order to satisfy the whims of fashion. Queen Victoria showed an interest in the spitz in 1888. Within ten years breeders had succeeded in breeding from large white dogs weighing at least 25 pounds or so, a smaller version weighing only four pounds with a choice of twelve different hues. The miniature spitz is the most sought after of all the spitz, but its popularity has suffered from the competition offered by the Pekingese. This reduction of its size has involved several modifications in its appearance: the skull is more domed, and the stop more prominent. The tail is not carried gaily, but flat against the back. On the other hand, its character has not changed and the miniature spitz is still as boisterous and noisy as its larger cousins. Plain coats should be uniform and of a clear hue. Markings on the coat should be in a regular pattern.

tan or mahogany. It is an intelligent and attractive animal and makes an excellent watchdog.

The miniature Pinscher is a smaller version of the Pinscher, measuring between 10 and 12 inches. It has all the qualities of the Pinscher and is much

1. Toy Spitz.
2.–3. Pomeranian Spitz.

Bichons

The bichons are descended from the barbets. They are toy dogs of Mediterranean origin, which have been in existence since time immemorial.

The Maltese bichon has a long body, round head and deep-set eyes, not protruding. It has short, straight legs. Fannius Strabo (Roman historian) tells us of a town in Sicily, Melita, renowned for the beauty of its toy dogs, which he called *canis Melitei*. These dogs could be the ancestors of the Maltese bichon, which has no connection with the island of Malta. The fringed tail is well arched over the back. All colours are permissible, but most Maltese dogs are white. The silky, abundant hair falls right to the ground and should not show any trace of waviness. The smallest Maltese bichons are the most popular. Their height should never exceed nine inches, and their weight should not be more than nine pounds.

The Tenerife dog or curly-haired bichon dates back to the 15th century. It is probably the product of a cross between the Maltese bichon and a small barbet. They are still known as Tenerife dogs, even though the breed has long since disappeared from the Canary Islands. The Curly-haired bichon has a wider skull than the Maltese bichon. Its coat is always white. The hair is curly

4. *Toy Spitz.*
5. *Tenerife dog.*
6. *Maltese Bichons.*

and woolly, never twisted. It can measure up to 12 inches and its weight ranges from five to nine pounds.

The Bolognese dog measures less than 12 inches. Its woolly hair is very thick all over the body, except on the muzzle. Its slightly erect ears are covered with hair. Its body is not quite so solid as that of the other bichons. Its weight should not exceed 11 pounds.

The Havanese dog, measuring 14 inches in height, is the largest of the bichons. Its flat, silky hair is completely white. Some authors accept chestnut or beige coats as permissible, as well as markings on the ears and flanks. Despite its name, it is of Mediterranean origin, like the other bichons, and it was the Spanish navigators who first introduced it into the Antilles.

Toys

Toy dogs are the smallest of the canine breeds. Despite their miniature size, they are just as capable of affection and loyalty as their larger cousins and they don't know the meaning of fear. Provided they are well looked after, they are not as fragile as their appearance would suggest, but they are not very prolific. They often have difficulty in giving birth and pure bred puppies sometimes fetch very high prices. Their classification within one group has been officially accepted in Britain and the United States.

The Chihuahua is the tiniest of all the dogs. It measures six to eight inches tall and weighs one to six pounds. It is of Mexican origin and was, it seems, considered sacred by the Aztecs. The aristocratic Aztec families reared hundreds of them, each dog having its own individual slave to serve it.

Bas-reliefs of the period show that the Chihuahua was already in existence in Central America in the 9th century A.D., although its height was greater then than it is today, and its coat less varied. The modern Chihuahua has a very domed skull, a pointed muzzle, large, almost black, globular eyes and slightly oblique, erect ears. The legs look rather thin. It has short, fine and dense hair. The coat can be whitish, steel blue or two or three of these hues.

There is also a long-haired variety, bred fairly recently, which was probably produced by crossing the short-haired variety with a miniature spaniel at some time. It has fringed ears and a bushy tail, and the hair, flat or slightly wavy, forms a noticeable ruff.

The Chihuahua is an intelligent animal which, despite its delicate appearance, has a lively, bold temperament.

The toy terrier is the miniature version of the black and tan terrier. It measures less than ten inches tall. Its weight should not exceed seven pounds, and the smallest-sized animals are the most sought after. The head is distinctly wedge-shaped with a flat skull and only a

slight stop. The ears are cornet-shaped and, except in Britain, are cropped to a point. The body is short, the back slightly arched and the legs very straight. The hair is dense, short and glossy. The coat is black with tan markings.

In spite of its small size, the toy terrier has the courage and aggressiveness typical of all terriers, and has no hesitation in attacking rats as big as itself. It is an elegant, affectionate dog.

The amertoy is a small, specifically American terrier. It is the product, it seems, of a cross between the Chihuahua and the Manchester terrier. It is very popular in the United States, although still not officially accepted by the Kennel Club. It has the physical and temperamental characteristics of a true terrier. It has a round skull, a pointed muzzle, a very black nose and small, erect ears. The large protruding eyes are inherited from the Chihuahua. Its hair is short and very thick. All hues, other than white, are permissible.

1. *Chihuahuas.*
2. *Toy Terrier.*
3. *Silky Terrier.*
4. *Yorkshire Terrier.*
5. *Toy Poodles.*

about slight modifications in the specific characteristics of the poodle. The head, in particular, often has the typical appearance of miniature breeds: bulging forehead and protruding eyes.

Dogs of Mixed Breed

Since all dogs belong to the same species, crosses between animals of different breeds produce fertile hybrids, which bear a certain resemblance to each of their parents.

Dogs of mixed breed are the product of crossbreeding between two different pure bred dogs or between a pure bred dog and a dog of no particular breed, or between two mongrels. In the past, crossbreeding was often deliberately tried in the creation of new breeds. By now, however, every possible combination has been tried by the breeders. They have experienced many setbacks but have also had some very fine successes to their credit, and there is little more to be expected from such crossbreeding. Today it is only resorted to if a certain breed is threatened with extinction. Then, in order to reconstitute it, breeders make use of another closely-related breed, with similar characteristics, in crosses. Subsequently, they are able to eliminate any traces of the related type by strict selective breeding. A breed may also be crossed with other breeds which had earlier helped to create it, in order to improve some specific characteristic such as speed or sense of smell.

In dogs, just as in every other kind of living being, ancestral influence decreases with every generation. The influence of each parent can be estimated as being 25 per cent, making a total of 50 per cent. In the fourth generation, when there would be a total of 16 ancestors, the contribution of each of these ancestors would fall to 0·78 per cent. One may assume, therefore, that from the tenth generation onwards, all foreign influence, whether accidental or otherwise, would be so diluted that there would be no need to take it into account. This is not the case, however. Heredity can reveal itself, at any moment, by crossing many generations in a single jump.

The Yorkshire terrier is the smallest of all the terriers. Its height should not exceed eight inches. It was first bred around 1850 by the weavers in the north of England. Its long, silky hair requires constant attention, especially for dogs that are exhibited at shows, whose coats need to be particularly thick. It is an intelligent and courageous animal, and makes an agreeable house companion, causing little trouble. It should not weigh more than seven pounds.

The Australian silky or Sydney silky has enjoyed great popularity in its native country for the last 25 years, and is now becoming more widespread throughout the world, especially in India and the United States. It is descended from the Yorkshire terrier, the Australian terrier and, to a lesser extent, from the Skye terrier. Its hair is very long and silky, its coat blue and tan, often with a darker mask. Its tail is docked. It measures eight to ten inches. tall and weighs eight to ten pounds.

The toy poodle is a miniature poodle, not accepted in France, but which is considered a separate breed in the United States. Its height should not exceed ten inches. The reduction in size has brought

Dogs of mixed breed, mostly the result of chance matings, are just as devoted, loyal and affectionate as their pure bred relatives.